KETO DESSERTS COOKBOOK 2019

110 Delicious and Easy to Make Ketogenic Dessert Recipes High-Fat, Low-Carb Desserts for Busy People Who Want To Lose Weight

ALBERTA FLOYD

TABLE OF CONTENTS

KETOGENIC CUSTARD RECIPES

KETO EGG CUSTARD

Prep Time: 5 minutes
Cooking Time: 30 minutes
Servings: 6

Nutritional Value (Estimated Amount Per Serving)

631 Calories
558 Calories from Fat
62g Total Fat
38g Saturated Fat
2g Trans Fat
3.4g Polyunsaturated Fat
16g Monounsaturated Fat
365mg Cholesterol
308mg Sodium
228mg Potassium
7.4g Total Carbohydrates
0.2g Dietary Fiber
7g Sugars
11g Protein

Ingredients

3 eggs, large
½ tsp. ground cinnamon
1 tbsp. vanilla
¼ cup Swerve or any granulated sweetener
2 cups heavy cream
¼ tsp. salt

Directions

1. Preheat your oven to 350 F in advance & bring a kettle filled with water to boil.
2. In a medium-sized bowl; beat the eggs until turn light yellow & foamy.
3. Add in the sweetener, cream, vanilla, cinnamon & salt; mix well.
4. Fill the custard cups with the prepared custard mixture; placing the cups either in a large cake pan or casserole dish. Fill the pan or dish with approximately an inch of hot water, preferably surrounding the cups.
5. Bake in the preheated oven until firm in the middle, for 30 minutes.

MOCHA CUSTARD

Prep Time: 5 minutes
Cooking Time: 10 minutes
Servings: 4

Nutritional Value (Estimated Amount Per Serving)

303 Calories
254 Calories from Fat
28g Total Fat
17g Saturated Fat
0.8g Trans Fat
1.6g Polyunsaturated Fat
7.9g Monounsaturated Fat
206mg Cholesterol
25mg Sodium
144mg Potassium
8.9g Total Carbohydrates
0.7g Dietary Fiber
7.2g Sugars
4.3g Protein

Ingredients

1 cup heavy/double cream
3 large egg yolks
½ cup coffee strong black
2 to 3 tbsp. dark chocolate, preferably 90%
1 tbsp. granulated sweetener of your choice or to taste

Directions

1. Gently warm the chocolate pieces together with cream and coffee over moderate heat settings in a small saucepan for a couple of minutes, until almost simmering (ensure

that you don't bring it to a boil). Remove the pan immediately from heat.
2. Whisk the eggs yolks with sweetener in a separate bowl for a minute or two, until pale & fluffy.
3. Slowly, whisk in the egg yolk mixture into the pan with the cream mixture, stirring continuously to stop the eggs from curdling or cooking.
4. Place the saucepan over low heat settings again & slowly whisk the mixture until thickens.
5. Pour the mixture into tiny espresso cups & refrigerate for a couple of hours, until completely set.

KETO CHOCOLATE CUSTARD

Prep Time: 10 minutes
Cooking Time: 10 minutes
Servings: 1

Nutritional Value (Estimated Amount Per Serving)

410 Calories
349 Calories from Fat
39g Total Fat
23g Saturated Fat
1.2g Trans Fat
2.1g Polyunsaturated Fat
10g Monounsaturated Fat
282mg Cholesterol
116mg Sodium
78mg Potassium
9.7g Total Carbohydrates
2.5g Dietary Fiber
1.8g Sugars
7g Protein

Ingredients

1 ½ tbsp. baking cocoa (sifted to reduce the chocolate lumps)
¼ cup heavy cream
1 tbsp. butter
5 tsp. swerve, confectioners
1 egg yolk

Directions

1. Over medium high heat settings in a small pot; heat the heavy cream until it starts forming bubbles. Immediately remove from the heat & decrease the heat settings to medium.
2. Stir in the butter until completely melted. Add in the swerve and sifted baking cocoa. Whisk until mixed thoroughly.
3. Add egg yolk to the pot & continue to whisk.
4. Put the pot on medium heat again & stir for a minute or two, until it starts to bubble & thicken. Remove from the heat and pour the mixture into a small cup or ramekin. Cover and let chill in a fridge until set, for an hour.
5. Serve chilled & enjoy.

KETO VANILLA CUSTARD

Prep Time: 15 minutes
Cooking Time: 5 minute
Servings: 5

Nutritional Value (Estimated Amount Per Serving)

783 Calories
716 Calories from Fat
80g Total Fat
48g Saturated Fat
2.4g Trans Fat
4.7g Polyunsaturated Fat
22g Monounsaturated Fat
658mg Cholesterol
124mg Sodium
226mg Potassium
7.8g Total Carbohydrates
0g Dietary Fiber
6.8g Sugars
12g Protein

Ingredients

6 large egg yolks
2 cups pure heavy whipping cream

1 vanilla bean (Sliced in half & scrape the seeds out using the back of a knife) or 2 tsp. vanilla extract
2 tbsp. granulated sweetener
A pinch of Salt

Directions

1. Over medium heat settings in a small-sized saucepan; add the vanilla bean together with seeds, cream & salt. Heat until it just starts boiling, stirring occasionally and then remove the pan from the heat.
2. In the meantime; whisk the egg yolks together with sweetener in a small-sized bowl for a minute or two, until combined well.
3. Slowly pour the hot cream mixture on top of the egg yolks; continue to whisk
4. Add the mixture to a clean saucepan & cook over medium-low heat until the mixture easily coats the back of a spoon and thickens, stirring continuously
5. Remove & strain to remove any lumps and the vanilla pod.

COCONUT CUSTARD

Prep Time: 10 minutes
Cooking Time: 50 minutes
Servings: 5

Nutritional Value (Estimated Amount Per Serving)

264 Calories
233 Calories from Fat
26g Total Fat
21g Saturated Fat
0g Trans Fat
0.8g Polyunsaturated Fat
2.1g Monounsaturated Fat
112mg Cholesterol
88mg Sodium
278mg Potassium
5.1g Total Carbohydrates
0.4g Dietary Fiber
1.6g Sugars
6g Protein

Ingredients

2 ¼ cups coconut milk
½ tsp. liquid stevia or 1/3 cup low-carb sweetener
A dash of ground nutmeg optional
3 large eggs
½ tsp. vanilla extract
2 tbsp. shredded coconut, unsweetened
A dash of salt

Directions

1. Whisk the eggs together with sweetener & salt in a large bowl until just blended.
2. Over moderate heat settings in a large saucepan; heat the coconut milk until it just starts to simmer.
3. Gradually whisk the heated coconut milk into the egg mixture.
4. Stir in the shredded coconut and vanilla extract.
5. Pour the mixture into five custard cups & sprinkle with the nutmeg, if desired.
6. Place cups in a large sized baking pan, preferably 13×9". Add approximately an inch of hot water to the pan.
7. Bake until a knife comes out clean, for 45 to 50 minutes, at 350 F.
8. Remove the cups to a wire rack & set aside for an hour to cool. Cover & store in the refrigerator until ready to serve.

LOW CARB RASPBERRY CUSTARD

Prep Time: 15 minutes
Cooking Time: 30 minutes
Servings: 4

Nutritional Value (Estimated Amount Per Serving)

463 Calories
384 Calories from Fat
43g Total Fat
25g Saturated Fat
1.2g Trans Fat

2.7g Polyunsaturated Fat
12g Monounsaturated Fat
389mg Cholesterol
39mg Sodium
144mg Potassium
8g Total Carbohydrates
0.9g Dietary Fiber
13g Sugars
7g Protein

Ingredients

1 cup Brut Champagne
1/3 cup Swerve Confectioners or Icing Sugar
2 ounces fresh raspberries
¼ tsp. stevia glycerite
6 egg yolks, large
1 2/3 cups heavy cream
¼ tsp. vanilla bean powder or ½ tsp. vanilla extract

Directions

1. Preheat your oven to 350 F in advance & place a rack to the center position. Over medium low to low heat settings in a large saucepan; heat the champagne heat until reduced to 2-3 tbsp. (ensure that you don't burn it). Pour into a glass bowl, preferably small-sized to cool.
2. Heat water in a tea kettle for a couple of minutes, until hot but not boiling. Add 1 tablespoon of the sweetener & the yolks to a medium-sized bowl. Beat well to break up the yolks completely; feel free to remove any chalazae that still remain. Add the heavy cream to a small-sized pot & add the vanilla bean powder and leftover sweetener. Place the pot over medium heat settings & cook for a couple of minutes, until bubbles start to simmer around the edge of the pot, stirring occasionally with a whisk. Turn off the heat settings & start pouring the egg yolk into the hot cream mixture (slowly in a thin stream, and continue to whisk). Whisk in the Stevia glycerite and reduced champagne.
3. Place 3 raspberries in each ramekin. Evenly divide the prepared crème brulee mixture

among 4 ramekins; placing the ramekins into the pan & fill the pan with hot water (approximately half way up the sides of the ramekins). Place the pan carefully into the oven & bake until the center of the crème brulee is set but still soft, for half an hour.
4. Before removing the crème brulee to a rack to cool completely; let them cool in the water bath for an hour. Using a plastic wrap; cover & let refrigerate for 4 hours or for overnight.
5. Just before serving, don't forget to sprinkle approximately ½ tsp. of sweetener over each of the crème brulee. Using a culinary torch; melt the sweetener until it caramelizes, turning brown and then, add a dollop of the whipped cream over the top. Garnish with more of fresh raspberries, if desired. Serve and enjoy.

WHOLE EGG ALMOND MILK CUSTARD

Prep Time: 2 minutes
Cooking Time: 10 minutes
Servings: 2

Nutritional Value (Estimated Amount Per Serving)

111 Calories
33 Calories from Fat
3.6g Total Fat
0.9g Saturated Fat
0g Trans Fat
0.8g Polyunsaturated Fat
1.7g Monounsaturated Fat
93mg Cholesterol
42mg Sodium
77mg Potassium
15g Total Carbohydrates
0.3g Dietary Fiber
10g Sugars
3.7g Protein

Ingredients

- 1 tbsp. maple syrup
- 1 large egg
- 1 cup almond milk
- 1 tbsp. corn starch or tapioca starch (arrowroot)

For Vanilla custard:

Add 1 teaspoon vanilla extract or 1 split of the vanilla bean during the cooking process

For Chocolate custard:

Add a tablespoon of the cacao powder during the cooking process

For Citrus custard:

Add a large piece of orange or lemon rind to the mixture during the cooking process

Directions

1. Whisk egg together with sweetener and starch in a large bowl for a couple of minutes, until completely smooth.
2. Slowly add in the almond milk and continue to whisk (try maintaining a smooth texture).
3. Slowly heat on the stove; continue to whisk for 5 more minutes, until the mixture thickens.
4. Remove from the heat; serve hot & enjoy.

CINNAMON CUSTARD RECIPE

Prep Time: 20 minutes
Cooking Time: 30 minutes
Servings: 6

Nutritional Value (Estimated Amount Per Serving)

404 Calories
334 Calories from Fat
37g Total Fat
23g Saturated Fat
1.2g Trans Fat
2g Polyunsaturated Fat
9.8g Monounsaturated Fat
219mg Cholesterol
56mg Sodium
124mg Potassium
13g Total Carbohydrates
0.1g Dietary Fiber
13g Sugars
5.8g Protein

Ingredients

- 2 large eggs, whole
- ½ tsp. cinnamon
- 2 cups heavy cream
- ½ cup sugar substitute such as liquid stevia
- 18 tsp. Caramel Flavored Syrup, sugar-free
- ½ tsp. vanilla extract
- 2 large egg yolks
- 1/8 tsp salt

Directions

1. Combine cream with cinnamon over medium heat settings in a medium-sized, heavy saucepan, whisking constantly to thoroughly blend the cinnamon into cream, until the cream just starts to steam. Ensure that you don't bring it to a boil. Immediately remove the pan from heat.
2. Preheat your oven to 300 F in advance.
3. Whisk the eggs together with egg yolks, sugar substitute & salt in a medium-sized bowl for a couple of minutes, until slightly thickened & turn pale yellow.
4. Continue to whisk & slowly pour in the hot cream using a soup ladle. Once you have added the entire cream, whisk in the vanilla extract.
5. Pour approximately ½ cup of the cream mixture into each of six custard cups, preferably 4-ounce each.
6. Place the cups in a roasting pan. Carefully pour enough of boiling water (approximately 4 cups) into the roasting pan.
7. Bake in the preheated oven for 25 to 30 minutes, until custard is still slightly soft in the middle..

8. Remove the cups carefully from water bath using an oven mitt.
9. Serve warm; topped each serving with approximately 1 tablespoon of the caramel syrup and enjoy.

SUMMER BLACKBERRY CUSTARDS

Prep Time: 15 minutes
Cooking Time: 45 minutes
Servings: 12

Nutritional Value (Estimated Amount Per Serving)

159 Calories
52 Calories from Fat
5.8g Total Fat
3.1g Saturated Fat
0.1g Trans Fat
0.6g Polyunsaturated Fat
1.5g Monounsaturated Fat
45mg Cholesterol
32mg Sodium
201mg Potassium
10g Total Carbohydrates
4g Dietary Fiber
17g Sugars
3.8g Protein

Ingredients

2 pounds blackberries (6 cups)
½ cup all-purpose flour
1 ½ cups whole milk
¾ cup packed dark brown sugar
2 large eggs
½ tsp. grated orange zest
1 tsp. pure vanilla extract
½ cup heavy cream
1 tbsp. lemon juice, freshly squeezed

Directions

1. Preheat your oven to 450 F in advance.
2. Spread ½ cup of the blackberries in each of 12 gratin dishes (4-ounce). Arrange the gratin dishes on two large-sized baking sheets.
3. Whisk the cream with eggs, milk, vanilla, flour, brown sugar, orange zest and lemon juice in a large bowl until completely smooth. Ladle approximately ¼ cup of the custard into each dish & bake in the preheated oven until the middle is just set, for 12 to 15 minutes. Transfer the custards to a wire rack & let stand for half an hour. Serve and enjoy.

KETO CHAI CHIA CUSTARD

Prep Time: 7 minutes
Cooking Time: 12 minutes
Servings: 1

Nutritional Value (Estimated Amount Per Serving)

228 Calories
100 Calories from Fat
11g Total Fat
1g Saturated Fat
0.1g Trans Fat
2.4g Polyunsaturated Fat
7.1g Monounsaturated Fat
0mg Cholesterol
252mg Sodium
550mg Potassium
33g Total Carbohydrates
5.4g Dietary Fiber
22g Sugars
3.3g Protein

Ingredients

1 ¾ cup almond milk, unsweetened, plain
1 tsp. vanilla extract
3 whole cloves
1 whole cinnamon stick
3 tbsp. whole pieces chia seeds
1 tbsp. ginger root, raw
2 Cardamom Pods, whole
1 tbsp. Xylitol

Directions

1. Add chia seeds with a cup of almond milk to a high-power blender. Blend on high settings until smooth
2. Add the leftover milk with the cloves, cardamom pods, ginger, vanilla, cinnamon and xylitol to a small-sized pan. Bring the milk to a simmer over low to medium heat settings (ensure that you don't bring it to a boil).
3. Add the blended chia mixture to the hot pan; thoroughly whisk until combined well; let simmer gently until thickened slightly.
4. Remove the milk from heat; set aside for a couple of minutes to let the spices to infuse.
5. Remove the whole spices from milk & pour the mixture into 2 separate ramekins.
6. Let cool until easy to handle and then transfer to a fridge; let chill. Serve with a little low-carb fruit or over the granola or enjoy on its own.

EASY SLOW COOKER LEMON CUSTARD

Prep Time: 10minutes
Cooking Time: 60minutes
Servings: 4

Nutritional Value (Estimated Amount Per Serving)

310 Calories
138 Calories from Fat
15g Total Fat
13g Saturated Fat
0g Trans Fat
0.6g Polyunsaturated Fat
1.8g Monounsaturated Fat
115mg Cholesterol
35mg Sodium
99mg Potassium
4g Total Carbohydrates
0.3g Dietary Fiber
20g Sugars
2.6g Protein

Ingredients

5 egg yolks, large
1 tsp. vanilla extract
¼ cup lemon juice, freshly squeezed
2 cups coconut cream or whipping cream
½ tsp. liquid stevia
Whipped coconut cream or whipped cream, lightly sweetened
1 tbsp. lemon zest

Directions

1. Whisk the egg yolks together with lemon zest, lemon juice, liquid stevia and vanilla in a medium bowl.
2. Whisk in the heavy cream & evenly divide the mixture among four jars or ramekins, small-sized.
3. Place a rack in the bottom of your slow cooker & place the ramekins over the rack. Add a few cups of water (enough to reach halfway up the sides of the ramekins).
4. Cover & cook for 3 hours on low-heat settings.
5. Remove the ramekins; set aside and let cool until easy to handle and then, let completely chill in a refrigerator. Just before serving; top with the whipped cream. Serve and enjoy.

KETOGENIC BROWNIES RECIPES

KETO AVOCADO BROWNIES

Prep Time: 5 minutes
Cooking Time: 30 minutes
Servings: 9

Nutritional Value (Estimated Amount Per Serving)

321 Calories
209 Calories from Fat
23g Total Fat
8.7g Saturated Fat
0.4g Trans Fat
2.5g Polyunsaturated Fat
9.4g Monounsaturated Fat
110mg Cholesterol
628mg Sodium
261mg Potassium
23g Total Carbohydrates
4.2g Dietary Fiber
15g Sugars
7.4g Protein

Ingredients

4 organic eggs, large
2 avocados, ripe
18 packets Stevia or 2/3 cup coconut sugar
2 tsp. baking soda
2/3 cup cocoa powder, unsweetened
6 tbsp. unsweetened peanut butter
1 stick (½ cup) butter, melted
2 tsp. pure vanilla extract
Flaky sea salt, optional
½ tsp. kosher salt

Directions

1. Line a standard-sized square pan, preferably 8x8" with the parchment paper and then, preheat your oven to 350 F in advance. Combine the entire ingredients (except flaky sea salt) together in a high power blended & blend on high settings until completely smooth.

2. Transfer the batter to prepared baking pan & smooth the top using a large spatula. If desired, feel free to top with the flaky sea salt.

3. Bake in the preheated oven for 20 to 25 minutes, until brownies are soft but still somewhat wet to the touch. Let cool for half an hour; slice into desired squares & serve.

NUT FREE KETO BROWNIE

Prep Time: 10 minutes
Cooking Time: 20 minutes
Servings: 12

Nutritional Value (Estimated Amount Per Serving)

140 Calories
114 Calories from Fat
13g Total Fat
7g Saturated Fat
0.2g Trans Fat
0.8g Polyunsaturated Fat
3.5g Monounsaturated Fat
112mg Cholesterol
143mg Sodium
58mg Potassium
2.3g Total Carbohydrates
0.2g Dietary Fiber
1.3g Sugars
4.2g Protein

Ingredients

6 medium eggs
1 to 2 tbsp. unsweetened cocoa
3 to 4 tbsp. melted butter
1 cup softened cream cheese
2 tsp vanilla
½ tsp. baking powder
4 tbsp. granulated sweetener, any of your choice or to taste

Directions

1. Put the entire ingredients together in a large-sized mixing bowl & blend using a stick blender with the blade attachment until completely smooth.
2. Pour the prepared mixture into a lined square baking dish (preferably 8 ½").
3. Bake until cooked on the middle, for 20 to 25 minutes, at 350F.
4. Slice into your favorite shapes such as rectangle, squares, bars or triangle wedges.

PEANUT BUTTER BROWNIES

Prep Time: 15 minutes
Cooking Time: 20 minutes
Servings: 16

Nutritional Value (Estimated Amount Per Serving)

186 Calories
148 Calories from Fat
16g Total Fat
7g Saturated Fat
0.3g Trans Fat
2.2g Polyunsaturated Fat
5.5g Monounsaturated Fat
22mg Cholesterol
151mg Sodium
121mg Potassium
7.5g Total Carbohydrates
1.3g Dietary Fiber
2.5g Sugars
4g Protein

Ingredients

For Brownie Base:

   1 recipe Ultimate Keto Brownies

For Chocolate Glaze:

   1 ½ ounces unsweetened chocolate, chopped finely
   ¼ tsp vanilla extract
   3 tbsp Swerve Sweetener, powdered
   ½ cup heavy whipping cream

For Peanut Butter Fudge:

   ¾ cup sifted Swerve Sweetener, powered
   ½ tsp vanilla
   6 tbsp butter
   ¾ cup peanut butter
   ¼ tsp salt

Directions

For Brownies:

1. For easy removal; line a standard-sized baking pan, preferably 8x8" with parchment paper with an overhang and prepare the keto brownie batter as mentioned on the package. Once done; pour the batter into the prepared pan & bake the brownies as mentioned; let cool for a couple of minutes in the pan.

For The Peanut Butter Fudge:

1. Over medium heat settings in a small saucepan; melt peanut butter together with normal butter and then stir in the vanilla & salt.
2. Slowly stir in the powdered Swerve until you get spreadable consistency and the mixture thickens. Spread over the cooled brownies & refrigerate until completely set, for an hour.

For Chocolate Glaze:

1. Now, heat the cream over moderate heat settings in a small saucepan until it just starts to simmer. Remove & add in the chopped chocolate. Let sit until completely melted, for 5 to 7 minutes.
2. Add the vanilla and sweetener; whisk until completely smooth. Let sit a couple of more minutes to thicken and then drizzle or spread over the peanut butter layer.
3. Lift the brownies out by edges of parchment paper & cut into desired squares.

FUDGY VEGAN KETO BROWNIES

Prep Time: 15 minutes
Cooking Time: 45 minute
Servings: 16

Nutritional Value (Estimated Amount Per Serving)

132 Calories
111 Calories from Fat
12g Total Fat
7.1g Saturated Fat
0g Trans Fat
1g Polyunsaturated Fat
3.4g Monounsaturated Fat
10mg Cholesterol
66mg Sodium
82mg Potassium
9g Total Carbohydrates
1.9g Dietary Fiber
0.3g Sugars
2.1g Protein

Ingredients

For the Flax Egg:

> 5 tbsp. coffee or water
> 2 tbsp. ground flaxseed (14g)

For Wet Ingredients:

> 1 tsp. pure vanilla extract
> 6 tbsp pure granulated stevia blend, (48g)
> 1/3 cup almond butter, unsweetened & unsalted (84g)
> 3 oz baking chocolate, unsweetened
> ¼ cup coconut oil (60g)

For Dry Ingredients:

> ½ tsp. xanthan gum
> ½ tsp. baking soda
> 1/3 cup cocoa powder (30g)
> ½ cup blanched almond flour (56g)
> ¼ tsp. Himalayan pink salt

Directions

1. Prepare the egg flax by whisking the ground flaxseed together with coffee or water in a bowl, preferably small-sized; set aside until you get gel like consistency.
2. Preheat your oven to 350 F in advance.
3. Combine the entire dry ingredients together in a large bowl; mix well & set aside until ready to use.
4. Now, over very low heat settings in a medium saucepan; melt the Pyure and baking chocolate, stirring constantly. Once melted; immediately remove from the heat & stir in the almond butter; mix well.
5. Finally, stir in the flax eggs, coconut oil and vanilla; continue to stir until smooth & combined well.
6. Stir the wet ingredients into the dry until well combined.
7. Line an 8x8" pan with parchment paper or grease/spray with the coconut oil. Spread the batter evenly into pan.
8. Bake in the preheated oven until a toothpick comes out clean, for 20 to 25 minutes.
9. Let completely cool and then transfer to a refrigerator to firm up. Once done, cut into 16 squares. Store in a freezer or refrigerator. Before serving; don't forget to warm the brownies at room temperature or enjoy as it.

DOUBLE CHOCOLATE BROWNIES

Prep Time: 20 minutes
Cooking Time: 45 minutes
Servings: 16

Nutritional Value (Estimated Amount Per Serving)

185 Calories
143 Calories from Fat
16g Total Fat
7.3g Saturated Fat

0g Trans Fat
2g Polyunsaturated Fat
5g Monounsaturated Fat
31mg Cholesterol
77mg Sodium
164mg Potassium
9.3g Total Carbohydrates
3.3g Dietary Fiber
1.5g Sugars
4g Protein

Ingredients

For Chocolate Avocado Frosting:

> 2 to 4 tbsp. powdered Erythritol or 1 - 2 tbsp. yacon syrup
> 1/3 cup raw cacao
> 2 ripe avocados
> 1 tbsp. virgin coconut oil
> ¼ tsp. vanilla powder

For Brownie Layer:

> ½ cup plus 2 tbsp. Swerve or powdered Erythritol
> 3 eggs, medium
> 1 cup almond flour (3.5 oz)
> ½ cup virgin coconut oil, melted
> 2 tsp. baking powder, gluten-free
> ½ cup plus 2 tbsp. raw cacao powder (1.9 oz)
> 2 tbsp. ground chia seeds (16 g)
> ¼ cup almond milk, unsweetened (60 ml)
> 1 tsp. vanilla powder
> 10 drops of liquid stevia
> 1 heaped tbsp. of almond butter (1.1 oz)

Directions

1. Preheat your oven to 320 F in advance.
2. Whisk the eggs in a large bowl and then add in the stevia and erythritol; mix well. Add in the almond milk & melted coconut oil; whisk well.
3. Add in the cacao, ground almonds, gluten free baking powder, chia seeds, almond butter and vanilla; continue to mix until completely smooth. Line a large-sized baking tray with greaseproof paper and spoon in the brownie mix; leveling the edges. Bake until a skewer comes out clean, for 25 to 30 minutes.

4. Let completely cool. In the meantime, place the entire frosting ingredients together in a high speed food processor; blitz until smooth. Spoon the frosting over the brownie base; slice & serve.

ALMOND FLOUR BROWNIES

Prep Time: 6 minutes
Cooking Time: 15 minutes
Servings: 15

Nutritional Value (Estimated Amount Per Serving)

262 Calories
224 Calories from Fat
25g Total Fat
14g Saturated Fat
0g Trans Fat
2.4g Polyunsaturated Fat
6.6g Monounsaturated Fat
54mg Cholesterol
151mg Sodium
132mg Potassium
5.6g Total Carbohydrates
2g Dietary Fiber
0.9g Sugars
5.1g Protein

Ingredients

> 1 cup almond flour
> 2/3 cup erythritol or stevia
> 1 tbsp. cocoa powder
> ¼ tsp. baking soda
> ¼ tsp. salt

For Wet Ingredients:

> 2 large eggs
> 1/3 cup almond milk, unsweetened
> 1 tsp. pure vanilla extract
> ½ cup melted coconut oil

For Toppings:

> ¼ cup sliced almonds

Directions

1. Line a standard-sized pan, preferably 8x8" with the parchment paper and then, preheat your oven to 350 F in advance. Or grease a muffin pan (preferably small-sized) with some of the coconut oil, if making brownie bites.
2. Combine the entire dry ingredients together in a medium-sized bowl. Mix the entire wet ingredients together in a bowl, preferably large-sized; mix well. Add the mixture of dry ingredients simply into the mixture of wet ingredients; mix until well combined.
3. Bake in the preheated oven until a toothpick comes out clean, for 12 to 15 minutes. Sprinkle with sliced almonds. Let completely cool and then cut into desired shapes. Serve and enjoy.

CHEESECAKE BROWNIES

Prep Time: 10 minutes
Cooking Time: 30 minutes
Servings: 16

Nutritional Value (Estimated Amount Per Serving)

171 Calories
140 Calories from Fat
16g Total Fat
8.2g Saturated Fat
0g Trans Fat
1.1g Polyunsaturated Fat
5g Monounsaturated Fat
57mg Cholesterol
105mg Sodium
69mg Potassium
5.4g Total Carbohydrates
0.9g Dietary Fiber
3.1g Sugars
3.2g Protein

Ingredients

For Cheesecake Layer:

1 large egg yolk

3 tbsp. Swerve sweetener or any low-carb sweetener
½ tsp. vanilla extract
8 ounces cream cheese

For Brownie Layer:

2 large eggs
¼ cup Swerve sweetener or any low-carb sweetener
1 stick (½ cup) melted butter, unsalted
¾ tsp. SweetLeaf stevia drops
½ tsp. monk fruit liquid extract
1 tsp. vanilla extract
½ cup almond flour
3 tbsp. coconut flour
¼ cup cocoa powder, unsweetened
1/8 tsp. sea salt

Directions

1. Line a standard-sized baking pan, preferably 8x8" with parchment paper or grease it well and then preheat your oven to 350 F in advance.

For Brownie Layer:

1. Combine sweeteners together with butter, vanillia extract, cocoa & salt in a large bowl until combined well.
2. Whisk in the eggs and then fold in the flours; reserve approximately ¼ cup of the prepared batter and spread the leftover batter into the prepared pan.

For Cheesecake Layer:

1. Beat the cream cheese together with vanilla, sweetener & egg yolk until blended well.
2. Evenly spread the cream cheese mixture on top of the brownie layer.

Swirl:

1. Drop the kept-aside brownie batter on top of the cheesecake layer.
2. Swirl in using a large knife.

3. Bake in the preheated oven for 25 to 30 minutes and then transfer to a rack to completely cool.

KETO CARAMEL NUT CHOCOLATE BROWNIES

Prep Time: 30 minutes
Cooking Time: 30 minutes
Servings: 16

Nutritional Value (Estimated Amount Per Serving)

71 Calories
9.2 Calories from Fat
1g Total Fat
0.6g Saturated Fat
0g Trans Fat
0.1g Polyunsaturated Fat
0.3g Monounsaturated Fat
3.4mg Cholesterol
104mg Sodium
399mg Potassium
12g Total Carbohydrates
2.3g Dietary Fiber
9.5g Sugars
4.3g Protein

Ingredients

For The Caramel:

1/3 cup half & half
3 tbsp. salted butter
½ tsp. caramel flavoring
2 tbsp. bourbon
1/3 cup erythritol granulated sweetener
¼ tsp. xanthan gum

For The Brownies:

½ cup butter, melted
1 tbsp. coconut flour
¾ cup almond flour
1 tsp. vanilla extract
1/3 cup granulated erythritol sweetener such as Swerve
3 large eggs
1 egg yolk
¼ cup cocoa powder, good-quality
1 tsp. baking powder
2 tbsp chocolate flavored syrup, sugar free (such as davinci or torani style)
¼ cup 90% cocoa dark chocolate, chopped (or more)

To Assemble:

1/3 cup walnuts, chopped or any of your favorite nut

Directions

For The Brownies:

1. Preheat your oven to 375 F in advance.
2. Combine the almond flour together with melted butter, coconut flour, vanilla extract, sweetener, eggs (including the yolk), chopped chocolate, cocoa powder & chocolate flavored syrup in a bowl, preferably medium-sized.
3. Using your hands; lightly stir the ingredients together until completely combined (ensure that you don't whip or beat the ingredients). Pour the prepared mixture into an 8×8 square pan lined with foil or parchment.
4. Bake until the center no longer jiggles, for 12 to 15 minutes. Remove & let cool completely before slicing.

For The Caramel:

1. Over medium heat settings in a small saucepan; melt the sweetener together with butter.
2. Cook until it starts bubbling, for 2 to 3 minutes, stirring constantly.
3. Add the xanthan bourbon, half & half & caramel flavoring.
4. Continue to whisk & cook over medium heat settings for 3 to 5 more minutes.
5. As you cook, it would get darker in color.
6. The moment you get your desired color; immediately remove the pan from heat.
7. Let it cool slightly (it would thicken, as it cools).

To Serve:

1. Remove the brownies from pan & peel off the foil or parchment.
2. Add the cooled caramel to a small plastic zip-log baggie and then cut approximately 1/8" off of one of the bottom corners of the bag.
3. Squeeze the caramel gently on top of the brownies.
4. Evenly sprinkle with the chopped nuts.
5. Then cut into 2×2 squares brownies (16 in total)
6. Serve and enjoy.

CHOCOLATE AND COCONUT PUMPKIN BROWNIES

Prep Time: 15 minutes
Cooking Time: 30 minutes
Servings: 9

Nutritional Value (Estimated Amount Per Serving)

127 Calories
41 Calories from Fat
4.6g Total Fat
2.3g Saturated Fat
0g Trans Fat
0.7g Polyunsaturated Fat
0.9g Monounsaturated Fat
0mg Cholesterol
252mg Sodium
156mg Potassium
6g Total Carbohydrates
3.3g Dietary Fiber
9.6g Sugars
2.7g Protein

Ingredients

1 mashed banana, medium
½ cup pumpkin puree
2 tbsp. ground flax seed
½ cup cocoa powder
2 tbsp. pure maple syrup
½ cup almond milk
1 tsp. vanilla extract
2 tsp. baking powder
½ cup unsweetened desiccated coconut, shredded
1 tsp. cinnamon
¼ cup dairy-free miniature chocolate chips
More of coconut shreds (optional), for topping
1 tsp. sea salt
½ cup oat flour

Directions

1. Line a standard-sized baking pan, preferably 8x8" or 7x11" with wax or parchment paper and then, preheat your oven to 350 F in advance.
2. Mash the banana well in a medium-sized mixing bowl & then stir in almond milk and pumpkin puree. While whisking; add in the cocoa powder and then stir in the flax, maple, baking powder, vanilla, cinnamon & salt until combined well.
3. Mix in the oat flour and coconut then stir in until completely smooth. Pour the batter into the prepared pan & evenly sprinkle with the chocolate chips.
4. Bake in the preheated oven until the center doesn't jiggle, for 25 to 30 minutes. Remove from the oven & let cool for 10 minutes then cut into desired shapes. Serve and enjoy.

LEMON BROWNIES WITH COCONUT LEMON GLAZE

Prep Time: 20 minutes
Cooking Time: 30 minutes
Servings: 15

Nutritional Value (Estimated Amount Per Serving)

183 Calories
136 Calories from Fat
15g Total Fat
6.8g Saturated Fat
0g Trans Fat
2.1g Polyunsaturated Fat

5.3g Monounsaturated Fat
25mg Cholesterol
90mg Sodium
162mg Potassium
9.6g Total Carbohydrates
2.5g Dietary Fiber
6g Sugars
4.4g Protein

Ingredients

2 cups almond flour
½ tsp. baking soda
2½ tbsp. lemon juice, freshly squeezed
1 tbsp. arrowroot powder
2 large eggs, at room temperature
¼ cup coconut oil, melted
4 tbsp. raw honey
1 tbsp. lemon zest, fresh
2 tbsp. coconut butter
⅓ cup coconut milk, full fat
1 tsp. vanilla extract
¼ tsp. salt

For Coconut Lemon Glaze:

2 tbsp. full-fat coconut milk
½ tbsp. lemon juice, freshly squeezed
2 tsp. arrowroot powder
1 tsp. raw honey
2 tsp. lemon zest
2½ tsp. coconut butter

Directions

1. Preheat your oven to 350 F in advance.
2. Mix the almond flour together with baking soda, arrowroot powder & salt in a large bowl
3. Whisk the eggs together with lemon zest, lemon juice, coconut milk, coconut oil, honey, vanilla extract and coconut butter in a separate bowl
4. Add the entire dry ingredients into the wet; gently mix with a spatula or spoon until you get batter like consistency; ensure that you don't over-mix the ingredients.
5. Spread batter across the bottom of baking pan (preferably 8x8") lined with the parchment paper. Ensure that the paper covers all sides of your pan.
6. Bake for 20 to 25 minutes, until a toothpick comes out clean.
7. Set pan on a wire rack to completely cool.

For Coconut Lemon Glaze:

1. Whisk the entire ingredients for the coconut lemon glaze together in a large bowl and then, evenly spread the glaze on top of the cooled brownies.
2. Cut into desired squares; serve & enjoy.

CHOCOLATE COVERED STRAWBERRY BROWNIES

Prep Time: 15 minutes
Cooking Time: 25 minutes
Servings: 16

Nutritional Value (Estimated Amount Per Serving)

485 Calories
239 Calories from Fat
27g Total Fat
16g Saturated Fat
0g Trans Fat
1.7g Polyunsaturated Fat
6.2g Monounsaturated Fat
49mg Cholesterol
93mg Sodium
275mg Potassium
7g Total Carbohydrates
4.2g Dietary Fiber
17g Sugars
3.6g Protein

Ingredients

1 tsp. vanilla extract
¾ cups plus 2 tbsp. unsweetened cocoa powder
1¼ cups coconut sugar
½ cup almond flour
2 large eggs
½ cup plus 2 tbsp. coconut oil
1 cup dark chocolate chunks, optional
¼ tsp. salt

For The Topping:

 ⅓ cup cocoa powder
 1 cup strawberries, fresh, diced
 2 tbsp. sugar substitute
 ⅓ cup coconut oil

Directions

1. Line a standard-sized baking pan, preferably 8x8" with aluminum foil (leaving the overhang on sides and then spray with the cooking spray); set the pan aside and then preheat your oven to 325 F in advance.
2. Combine cocoa powder together with coconut oil, coconut sugar & salt in a large microwave-safe bowl; heat on high power for 40 to 45 seconds, until melted. Stop; give everything a good stir & then heat again until the mixture has melted & you can easily stir the mixture, in 10-second bursts. To help dissolving the coconut sugar into the oil; continue to whisk for half a minute more.
3. Add the eggs & vanilla; vigorously stir until batter is thick, shiny & blended well. Add in the almond flour; continue to stir until well combined. Pour the prepared batter into the pan & spread it out evenly.
4. Bake in the preheated oven for 22 to 25 minutes, until a toothpick in the center emerges slightly moist with batter. Once done; let the brownies to completely cool.
5. Evenly spread the strawberries on top of the brownies. Whisk the coconut oil together with maple syrup and cocoa powder in a small bowl. Evenly pour on top of the strawberries. Refrigerate for an hour and then cut into 16 even-sized squares.

KETOGENIC COOKIES RECIPES

KETO CHOCOLATE CHIP COOKIES

Prep Time: 10 minutes
Cooking Time: 30 minutes
Servings: 12

Nutritional Value (Estimated Amount Per Serving)

230 Calories
186 Calories from Fat
21g Total Fat
8.5g Saturated Fat
0.3g Trans Fat
2.2g Polyunsaturated Fat
8.2g Monounsaturated Fat
36mg Cholesterol
144mg Sodium
112mg Potassium
8.2g Total Carbohydrates
3g Dietary Fiber
0.9g Sugars
4.8g Protein

Ingredients

½ cup butter, salted
1 ½ cup almond meal
¾ cup chocolate chips, sugar-free
½ tsp. baking powder
1 large egg
¾ cup erythritol
½ tsp. xanthan gum, optional
1 tsp. vanilla extract
¼ tsp. Himalayan pink salt

Directions

1. Preheat your oven to 355 F in advance. Microwave the butter until completely melted, for 30 seconds (ensure that it's not hot).

2. Place the melted butter into a large-sized mixing bowl & beat with the erythritol. The next step is to add the egg and vanilla; mix on low for 15 to 20 more seconds.
3. Add in the almond flour, baking powder, xanthan gum & salt; continue to mix until combined well.
4. Press the dough together & immediately remove it from the bowl. Now, using your hands; combine the chocolate chips into the prepared dough.
5. Roll the dough to form 12 balls & then arrange them on a large-sized baking tray (flatten them just like shape of a cookie using the palm of your hand). Bake in the preheated oven for 10 to 12 minutes.
6. Let completely cool & then serve.

MINT CREAM KETO COOKIES

Prep Time: 25minutes
Cooking Time: 12 minutes
Servings: 15

Nutritional Value (Estimated Amount Per Serving)

234 Calories
61 Calories from Fat
6.8g Total Fat
4.1g Saturated Fat
0g Trans Fat
0.3g Polyunsaturated Fat
1.9g Monounsaturated Fat
16mg Cholesterol
204mg Sodium
72mg Potassium
40g Total Carbohydrates
2.4g Dietary Fiber
0.1g Sugars
3.5g Protein

Ingredients

1 cup erythritol or lakanto monk fruit classic sweetener
2 ¼ cups almond flour
1tsp. vanilla extract
4 oz Grass-fed butter, softened & unsalted
1 tsp. baking powder
4 tbsp. unsweetened cocoa powder
1 ½ tsp. Xanthan Gum
3 tbsp. coconut flour
1 large egg
4 oz cream cheese
1 tsp. peppermint extract

Directions

1. Preheat your oven to 350 F in advance.
2. Combine the almond flour together with baking powder, xanthan gum, coconut flour & salt in a medium-sized bowl; mix well.
3. Combine the Monk Fruit Classic sweetener together with ½ cup of butter in a separate bowl for a couple of minutes, until light & fluffy.
4. Add in the vanilla extract and egg; continue to mix.
5. Add the bowl with dry ingredients; mix until well combined
6. Place the dough between two waxed paper sheets & press/roll the dough out until approximately 1/8" thick. Using a round cutter; cut out the cookies as many as you possibly can. Repeat this step until you have utilized the dough completely. Arrange them onto a cookie sheet lined with parchment.
7. Place the cookie halves onto a cookie sheet lined with parchment & bake for 10 to 12 more minutes.
8. In the meantime, blend the cream cheese together with the leftover butter. Mix in the peppermint extract and vanilla extract. Mix in the leftover monk fruit classic sweetener
9. Once the cookies are cool and you can handle them easily; divide the cream evenly on top of the cookie halves; pressing

with another cookie half gently on top of all the halves with crème. Serve and enjoy.

KETO SHORTBREAD COOKIES

Prep Time: 20 minutes
Cooking Time: 15 minutes
Servings: 25

Nutritional Value (Estimated Amount Per Serving)

609 Calories
245 Calories from Fat
27g Total Fat
4.2g Saturated Fat
0g Trans Fat
3.1g Polyunsaturated Fat
17g Monounsaturated Fat
25mg Cholesterol
787mg Sodium
343mg Potassium
75g Total Carbohydrates
1.2g Dietary Fiber
2.1g Sugars
15g Protein

Ingredients

½ cup powdered erythritol
1 cup almond flour
½ tsp. xanthan gum
4 to 5 tbsp. grass-fed butter at room temperature
½ tsp. vanilla extract
¼ tsp. kosher salt

For Chocolate Coating

Melted dark chocolate like Lily's
Flakey sea salt

Directions

1. Toast the almond flour over medium heat settings in a dry pan or skillet for 3 to 5 minutes, until turn golden & fragrant. Remove the toasted flour from the pan and then whisk in the xanthan gum and salt; set aside to completely cool.

2. Now, in a large bowl; cream the butter for a couple of minutes using an electric mixer. Add in the sweetener & continue beating until mixed thoroughly & the sweetener has almost dissolved. Add in the vanilla extract & continue to beat until just combined, for a minute or two more.
3. With the mixer still on low settings; add in half of the almond flour mixture; continue to mix until just incorporated and then combine with the leftover almond flour mixture.
4. Wrap the cookie dough with saran wrap (cling film) & refrigerate for an hour.
5. Preheat your oven to 350 F in advance.
6. Roll the dough out between parchment paper & simply slice it with a sharp knife. Arrange the shaped cookies over the baking tray & place in the freezer for 12 to 15 minutes.
7. Bake in the preheated oven for 10 to 15 minutes, until turn lightly golden..
8. Let cool on the pan and then store them for up to a week in an airtight container.

CREAM CHEESE COOKIES

Prep Time: 15 minutes
Cooking Time: 15 minutes
Servings: 15

Nutritional Value (Estimated Amount Per Serving)

359 Calories
281 Calories from Fat
31g Total Fat
24g Saturated Fat
0.5g Trans Fat
0.8g Polyunsaturated Fat
4.6g Monounsaturated Fat
63mg Cholesterol
236mg Sodium
160mg Potassium
8g Total Carbohydrates
4.2g Dietary Fiber
7g Sugars
3.1g Protein

Ingredients

2 cup coconut flour
½ cup softened butter
1 large egg
½ cup Erythritol or any sugar substitute
3 tbsp. cream cheese softened
½ tsp. baking powder
1 tsp. Vanilla extract
¼ tsp. salt

Directions

1. Cream the butter together with erythritol and cream cheese in a large bowl. Add in the egg and vanilla extra. Beat for a couple of minutes, until completely smooth.
2. Add in the baking powder, coconut flour & salt; continue to beat until combined well and you get stick batter like consistency.
3. Place the prepared mixture on a piece of parchment or wax paper. Mould into a log shape & secure the ends.
4. Place in a fridge for an hour, until firm up.
5. Line a large-sized baking tray with the parchment paper and preheat your oven 350 F in advance.
6. Remove the dough from fridge & cut into slices, preferably 1 cm
7. Arrange the slices over the prepared baking tray.
8. Bake in the preheated oven until turn golden, for 15 to 18 more minutes.

LEMON SUGAR COOKIES

Prep Time: 10 minutes
Cooking Time: 50 minutes
Servings: 5

Nutritional Value (Estimated Amount Per Serving)

71 Calories
32 Calories from Fat
3.6g Total Fat
0.5g Saturated Fat
0g Trans Fat

0.4g Polyunsaturated Fat
2.5g Monounsaturated Fat
0mg Cholesterol
9.7mg Sodium
54mg Potassium
9.1g Total Carbohydrates
2.3g Dietary Fiber
0.2g Sugars
1.5g Protein

Ingredients

A batch of sugar cookie dough
¼ to ½ cup erythritol; blended into powder form
Juice and zest of 2 lemons, fresh

Directions

1. Knead the lemon zest in ¼ of batch & bake the cookies as per the directions mentioned on the package.
2. Once done; set aside and let cool. In the meantime, combine the erythritol together with lemon juice and prepare the icing. Spoon the prepared icing on top of the cooled cookies & place them in a freezer or fridge until the icing is set & chilled.

KETO OREO COOKIES

Prep Time: 15 minutes
Cooking Time: 30 minutes
Servings: 4

Nutritional Value (Estimated Amount Per Serving)

213 Calories
37 Calories from Fat
4.2g Total Fat
0.6g Saturated Fat
0g Trans Fat
0.7g Polyunsaturated Fat
2.6g Monounsaturated Fat
0mg Cholesterol
11mg Sodium
171mg Potassium
40g Total Carbohydrates

8.2g Dietary Fiber
0.6g Sugars
5.3g Protein

Ingredients

2 tbsp. softened butter or coconut oil
½ cup almond flour
2 tbsp. monk fruit sweetener
¼ tsp. baking soda
1 large egg
¼ cup cocoa powder

For Filling:

1 tbsp monk fruit sweetener
4 tbsp plain coconut butter
4 tbsp. plain coconut butter

Directions

1. Combine soften butter or coconut oil together with the egg and monk fruit; whisk until combined well. Add in the almond flour, cocoa powder & baking soda; continue to mix using a rubber spatula until thicken and you get dough like consistency. Wrap in a seran wrap & let refrigerate for an hour.
2. Remove & dust the counter with some cocoa powder & then dust the rolling pin in the cocoa powder as well.
3. Roll into a sheet approximately ¼" thick & punch out approximately 1 to 1½" circles. Bake at 275 F for 35 to 40 minutes.

For the Filling

1. Combine the coconut butter together with monk fruit using a rubber spatula for a couple of minutes, until combined well.

To Assemble:

1. Pull the cookies from oven; set aside & let them completely cool.
2. Spread approximately a teaspoon of the prepared filling on one cookie; pressing another on it (just like a sandwich). Serve and enjoy.

SOFT GINGERSNAP COOKIES

Prep Time: 10 minutes
Cooking Time: 15 minutes
Servings: 18

Nutritional Value (Estimated Amount Per Serving)

66 Calories
62 Calories from Fat
6.9g Total Fat
4.3g Saturated Fat
0.3g Trans Fat
0.3g Polyunsaturated Fat
1.8g Monounsaturated Fat
28mg Cholesterol
109mg Sodium
21mg Potassium
3.9g Total Carbohydrates
0g Dietary Fiber
0.7g Sugars
0.5g Protein

Ingredients

1 large egg
½ cup gentle sweet
3 "doonks" Pure Stevia
½ cup butter softened
2 tsp. un-sulphured blackstrap molasses
¼ tsp. cinnamon
2 tsp. ginger powder
1 ¼ cups healthy mama baking blend
½ tsp. salt

For Frosting:

1 tbsp. gentle sweet
3 tbsp. heavy whipping cream
1 tbsp. softened butter

Directions

1. Preheat your oven to 325 F in advance.
2. Cream the softened butter together with Gentle Sweet & stevia extract in a large-sized mixing bowl.
3. Add molasses and egg; continue to mix until combined well.
4. Add in the leftover ingredients & continue to mix until well blended.
5. Place the cookies on a large-sized cookie sheet lined with parchment using a cookie scoop & slightly flatten them using your fingers.
6. Bake in the preheated oven for 12 to 15 minutes. Remove & completely cool.

For Frosting:

1. Combine the softened butter together with heavy whipping cream and Gentle Sweet with a hand mixer for a minute or two, until just starting to stiffen. Spread a few teaspoons of the frosting on each cookie & store them in a refrigerator, in an airtight container for upto a week.

KETO PEANUT BUTTER COOKIES

Prep Time: 15 minutes
Cooking Time: 20 minutes
Servings: 16

Nutritional Value (Estimated Amount Per Serving)

54 Calories
39 Calories from Fat
4.3g Total Fat
0.9g Saturated Fat
0g Trans Fat
1g Polyunsaturated Fat
1.8g Monounsaturated Fat
12mg Cholesterol
47mg Sodium
52mg Potassium
2.6g Total Carbohydrates
0.5g Dietary Fiber
0.6g Sugars
2.2g Protein

Ingredients

½ cup peanut butter
1 large egg
½ cup Swerve or erythritol, powdered

Directions

1. Line a large-sized baking sheet with the parchment paper and then preheat your oven to 350 F in advance.
2. Combine the entire ingredients together in a large-sized mixing bowl & mix with a spatula for a couple of minutes, until combined well.
3. Scoop the dough out & make balls using a 1 ½ tbsp cookie scoop. Arrange them on the baking sheet; pressing the balls with a large fork (forming a criss-cross pattern). Bake in the preheated oven until the tops are set & turn golden, for 12 to 15 minutes.
4. Let the cookies to cool for 8 to 10 minutes at room temperature

GIRL SCOUT COOKIES

Prep Time: 40 minutes
Cooking Time: 10 minutes
Servings: 32

Nutritional Value (Estimated Amount Per Serving)

120 Calories
95 Calories from Fat
11g Total Fat
2.8g Saturated Fat
0.1g Trans Fat
2g Polyunsaturated Fat
4.8g Monounsaturated Fat
5.8mg Cholesterol
55mg Sodium
108mg Potassium
4.3g Total Carbohydrates
1.5g Dietary Fiber
1.1g Sugars
3.5g Protein

Ingredients

For Shortbread Cookie Layer

1 tsp. vanilla extract
2 ½ cup blanched almond flour
½ cup powdered Erythritol

6 tbsp softened butter, at room temperature

For Peanut Butter Layer:

¾ cup unsweetened peanut butter
2 tbsp erythritol, powdered or to taste

For Chocolate Coating:

1 tbsp. coconut oil
10 oz dark chocolate chips, sugar-free

Directions

1. *For The Shortbread Cookies:* Line a large-sized cookie sheet with the parchment paper and then preheat your oven to 350 F in advance.
2. Beat the butter together with erythritol using a stand mixer or hand mixer until light in color & fluffy.
3. Beat in the vanilla extract and then slowly beat the almond flour.
4. Scoop rounded tablespoonfuls of the prepared dough onto the cookie sheet. Flatten the cookies to approximately .8 cm (1/3") thick.
5. Bake in the preheated oven until the edges turn golden, for 10 to 12 minutes. Let completely cool in the pan.
6. Now, blend or stir the powdered erythritol together with peanut butter. (Feel free to adjust the amount of sweetener to taste). Spread a tsp. of the mixture over each cookie and then arrange the cookies onto the baking sheet lined with parchment again; freeze until the peanut butter is completely solid, for at a couple of hours.
7. Now, in a medium bowl; combine the chocolate chips with coconut oil; mix well. Heat in the microwave until melted completely, stirring after every 10 to 15 seconds intervals.
8. Using a large fork; dip each cookie into the prepared chocolate and coat all sides of your cookies. Shake the excess off and then arrange them onto the baking sheet lined with parchment again. Repeat this step with the leftover cookies. Let completely cool & let the chocolate to solidify before serving. Enjoy.

COCONUT CHIP COOKIES

Prep Time: 15 minutes
Cooking Time: 12 minutes
Servings: 16

Nutritional Value (Estimated Amount Per Serving)

191 Calories
151 Calories from Fat
17g Total Fat
6.4g Saturated Fat
0.2g Trans Fat
2.3g Polyunsaturated Fat
6.9g Monounsaturated Fat
35mg Cholesterol
72mg Sodium
176mg Potassium
4g Total Carbohydrates
2.9g Dietary Fiber
2.8g Sugars
4.9g Protein

Ingredients

¼ cup melted butter
½ cup coconut flakes, unsweetened
2 large eggs
½ cup cacao nibs
1 cup almond flour
½ cup almond butter
20 drops of liquid Stevia
1/3 cup erythritol
¼ tsp. salt

Optional Glaze Ingredients:

¼ cup heavy whipping cream
½ tsp. vanilla extract
10 drops of Liquid Stevia
1/8 tsp. guar gum

Directions

1. Preheat your oven to 350 F in advance. Combine the entire dry ingredients such as unsweetened coconut flakes, erythritol, almond flour, cacao nibs & salt together in a large bowl.

2. Melt the butter in a microwave and then combine the entire wet ingredients together: such as melted butter, almond butter, liquid stevia and eggs. Feel free to add the optional vanilla extract at this step.

3. Slowly pour the mixture of dry ingredients into the mixture of wet ingredients and thoroughly mix.

4. Spoon out evenly spaced cookies on a silpat or a baking sheet lined with parchment paper.

5. Using your fingers; flatten the cookie dough to approximately 1/3" thick.

6. Bake in the preheated oven until the edges turn golden brown, for 20 to 25 minutes. Remove & place them on a cooling rack to completely cool.

7. Now, prepare a glaze by mixing the heavy cream together with sweetener & extract using an immersion blender or a small mixer. While blending; slowly add in the guar gum until thickens.

8. Glaze the top of your cookies and refrigerate for a couple of hours. Serve and enjoy!

SNICKERDOODLE COOKIES

Prep Time: 10 minutes
Cooking Time: 12 hours
Servings: 16

Nutritional Value (Estimated Amount Per Serving)

262 Calories
205 Calories from Fat
23g Total Fat
7.6g Saturated Fat
0g Trans Fat
3.9g Polyunsaturated Fat
9.6g Monounsaturated Fat
23mg Cholesterol
103mg Sodium
353mg Potassium
5g Total Carbohydrates
4.8g Dietary Fiber

3.8g Sugars
7.3g Protein

Ingredients

- 2 large eggs
- 1 cup almond butter
- ¼ cup solid coconut oil, at room temperature
- 2 tsp. vanilla extract
- ½ cup almond milk
- 1 ½ cup monk fruit sweetener
- 1 cup coconut flour
- 1 ¾ cup almond flour
- 1 tsp. cinnamon
- 2 tsp. cream of tartar
- 1 tsp. baking soda
- 1/8 tsp. pink Himalayan salt

For The Coating:

- 1 tbsp cinnamon
- 3 tbsp monk fruit sweetener

Directions

1. Line a large-sized baking sheet with the parchment paper and then preheat your oven to 350 F in advance.
2. Combine eggs together with almond milk, almond butter, vanilla extract & coconut oil in a bowl, preferably medium-sized using an electric mixer.
3. Whisk the entire dry ingredients together in a separate bowl. Work in batches & add the dry ingredients to the wet ingredients; continue to mix using your hands until completely incorporated.
4. Place the batter bowl in a refrigerator for 15 minutes and let chill. Once done, make small-sized balls from the prepared batter; rolling each ball into the cinnamon sugar coating mixture & then arrange them on the prepared baking sheet.
5. Flatten balls into cookies like shape using the bottom of a glass or the palm of your hand. Bake in the preheated oven for 10 to 12 minutes.
6. Remove & let slightly cool before serving.

ALMOND CINNAMON BUTTER COOKIES

Prep Time: 10minutes
Cooking Time: 12 hour
Servings: 12

Nutritional Value (Estimated Amount Per Serving)

186 Calories
157 Calories from Fat
17g Total Fat
5.7g Saturated Fat
0.3g Trans Fat
2.7g Polyunsaturated Fat
8g Monounsaturated Fat
36mg Cholesterol
67mg Sodium
146mg Potassium
5.1g Total Carbohydrates
2.4g Dietary Fiber
1.6g Sugars
4.6g Protein

Ingredients

- 1 large egg
- 2 cups blanched almond flour
- ½ cup softened butter, at room temperature
- 1 tsp. vanilla extract, sugar-free
- ½ cup natural sweetener, low-calorie (like Swerve)
- 1 tsp. ground cinnamon

Directions

1. Line a large-sized baking sheet with the parchment paper and then, preheat your oven to 350 F in advance.
2. Combine the almond flour together with sweetener, egg, butter, cinnamon & vanilla extract in a large bowl; continue to mix until combined well.
3. Roll the dough into 1" thick balls. Arrange them on the prepared baking sheet; pressing down slightly with a fork twice, preferably in a crisscross pattern.

4. Now, bake for 12 to 15 minutes, until edges turn golden. Let the cookies to cool on the baking sheet for a minute and then remove to a wire rack to completely cool. Serve and enjoy.

OATMEAL COOKIES

Prep Time: 15minutes
Cooking Time: 14 hour
Servings: 20

Nutritional Value (Estimated Amount Per Serving)

526 Calories
269 Calories from Fat
30g Total Fat
7.9g Saturated Fat
0g Trans Fat
3.6g Polyunsaturated Fat
17g Monounsaturated Fat
16mg Cholesterol
189mg Sodium
581mg Potassium
57g Total Carbohydrates
5.9g Dietary Fiber
8.6g Sugars
11g Protein

Ingredients

For Cream:

1/3 cup Sukrin Gold or brown sugar sub
4 oz softened butter, unsalted
½ tsp. vanilla extract

For Whisk:

¾ tsp cinnamon
1 cup almond flour
2 tsp grass-fed beef gelatin
¼ tsp baking soda
2 tbsp oat fiber
¼ tsp salt

Other Ingredients:

1 ½ cups sliced almonds
1 large egg, cold

Directions

1. Place the rack into the center of your oven and preheat your oven to 350 F in advance. Line a sheet pan with the parchment paper. Chop the sliced almonds in a food processor until you get the size like oats. Measure out the dry ingredients & whisk them well; removing any lumps that you can see.
2. Cream the softened butter together with vanilla extract & Sukrin Gold for a minute or two, until light & fluffy; scrapping down the sides of your bowl, as required.
3. Add the entire dry ingredients together & continue to beat for a minute more, until combined well. Add in the egg & beat until combined well. Fold in the chopped sliced almonds.
4. Scoop the dough out using a 2 tbsp. cookie scoop & place them approximately 2" apart on the prepared cookie sheet.
5. Bake in the preheated oven for 7 to 10 minutes; remove & bang the cookie sheet gently on the stove for a couple of times. Place in the oven again and continue to bake for 6 more minutes.
6. Remove & smack each cookie lightly with a large spatula. Let cool for 5 minutes and then remove to a wire rack to completely cool. Serve and enjoy.

KETOGENIC CUPCAKE RECIPES

CHOCOLATE CUPCAKES

Prep Time: 30 minutes
Cooking Time: 60 minutes
Servings: 14

Nutritional Value (Estimated Amount Per Serving)

139 Calories
101 Calories from Fat
11g Total Fat
4.2g Saturated Fat
0.2g Trans Fat
1.4g Polyunsaturated Fat
4.4g Monounsaturated Fat
56mg Cholesterol
232mg Sodium
92mg Potassium
4.5g Total Carbohydrates
1.8g Dietary Fiber
0.7g Sugars
5.3g Protein

Ingredients

¼ cup unflavored protein powder
1 tsp. xanthan gum
2/3 cup cocoa powder, unsweetened
1 tsp. baking soda
6 tbsp. butter, room temperature
1 cup Swerve, Granular
¼ cup unsweetened almond milk
1 tbsp. apple cider vinegar
3 large eggs, room temperature
1 cup almond flour
¼ cup sour cream
1 tbsp. vanilla extract
½ tsp. salt

Directions

1. Line two standard-sized muffin pans with liners and then preheat your oven to 350 F in advance.
2. Stir the almond flour together with cocoa powder, baking powder, protein powder, xanthan gum & salt in a medium mixing bowl; mix well & set aside until ready to use.
3. Combine vinegar with baking soda in a small bowl. Mix well & set aside as well.
4. Add the Swerve and softened butter in a large bowl. Cream for 5 minutes using an electric mixer. Add in the eggs, sour cream & vanilla extract; continue to mix over medium speed settings. Add the dry mixture followed by almond milk & vinegar mixture; continue to mix until combined well, for 3 more minutes.
5. Evenly pour the batter into the muffin liners; filling them approximately ¾ full.
6. Bake in the preheated oven until a toothpick comes out clean, for 20 to 25 minutes.
7. Let cool for a couple of minutes and then remove to a wire rack to completely cool.
8. Frost your cupcakes with the chocolate butter-cream frosting; serve and enjoy.

KETO VANILLA CUPCAKE

Prep Time: 20 minutes
Cooking Time: 25 minutes
Servings: 16

Nutritional Value (Estimated Amount Per Serving)

206 Calories
173 Calories from Fat
19g Total Fat
8.5g Saturated Fat
0.1g Trans Fat
2.3g Polyunsaturated Fat
7.3g Monounsaturated Fat
70mg Cholesterol

248mg Sodium
158mg Potassium
6g Total Carbohydrates
2.4g Dietary Fiber
1.3g Sugars
5.5g Protein

Ingredients

2 cup blanched almond flour
1 tsp. baking soda
2/3 cup organic coconut flour
1 tbsp. baking powder
½ cup softened butter, unsalted (1 stick)
1 tsp. Xanthan Gum
4 large eggs, at room temp
1 cup Pyure organic stevia blend
2 tsp. vanilla extract
½ cup heavy whipping cream, at room temp
4 drops of liquid stevita, organic
1 tsp. apple cider vinegar, organic
2 large egg whites, at room temp
½ tsp. Himalayan pink salt

Directions

1. Begin the process by bringing heavy whipping cream, eggs plus egg whites & butter to room temperature.
2. In the meantime; preheat your oven to 350 F in advance.
3. Whisk Blanched almond flour, coconut flour, baking powder, baking soda, Xanthan gum & Himalayan pink salt in a medium-sized bowl; whisk until completely blended and no clumps remain; set aside.
4. Add sweetener and butter in a large mixing bowl. Continue to beat until creamed.
5. Add eggs plus the whites; whisk for a minute or two, until incorporated well.
6. Add in the apple cider vinegar, heavy whipping cream, liquid stevia and vanilla; blend well.
7. Add the dry mixture to the wet; thoroughly mix until well incorporated.
8. Scoop the batter into a gallon-sized ziplock bag using a large spatula or into a piping bag.

9. Pipe the batter into each greased muffin liner, approximately 2/3 full.
10. Release any trapped air bubbles by tapping the tray on the counter.
11. Bake each tray in the preheated oven for 20 to 25 minutes

KETO COCONUT FLOUR CUPCAKES

Prep Time: 15 minutes
Cooking Time: 35 minutes
Servings: 12

Nutritional Value (Estimated Amount Per Serving)

240 Calories
165 Calories from Fat
18g Total Fat
13g Saturated Fat
0.3g Trans Fat
0.8g Polyunsaturated Fat
3.3g Monounsaturated Fat
87mg Cholesterol
202mg Sodium
87mg Potassium
7g Total Carbohydrates
0.9g Dietary Fiber
13g Sugars
3.2g Protein

Ingredients

4 large eggs
2/3 cups coconut flour
1 cup erythritol
2 tsp. baking powder
1 cup coconut cream
2 ounces cream cheese
1 tsp. vanilla extract
½ cup butter

Directions

1. Line a standard-sized cupcake tin (preferably with 12 cups) with liners and then preheat your oven to 350 F in advance.

2. In a large bowl; combine coconut flour with baking powder; set aside until ready to use.
3. Cut the butter into small squares & put in another bowl; add in the cream cheese & microwave the cream cheese & butter for half a minute. Keep an eye on everything; don't let it burn, stirring frequently until combined well.
4. Add in the vanilla extract, erythritol & coconut cream to the butter-cream cheese mixture; give everything a good stir.
5. Pour the wet ingredients into a large bowl with baking powder and coconut flour; stir well.
6. Slowly add eggs to the batter; stir well after each addition.
7. Pour the prepared batter into the cupcake tin; bake until a toothpick comes out clean, for 35 minutes.
8. Let completely cool. Serve and enjoy.

KETO STRAWBERRY CUPCAKES

Prep Time: 10 minutes
Cooking Time: 15 minute
Servings: 6

Nutritional Value (Estimated Amount Per Serving)

151 Calories
123 Calories from Fat
14g Total Fat
9.7g Saturated Fat
0.3g Trans Fat
0.5g Polyunsaturated Fat
2.5g Monounsaturated Fat
51mg Cholesterol
377mg Sodium
102mg Potassium
4g Total Carbohydrates
1.5g Dietary Fiber
1.3g Sugars
4g Protein

Ingredients

½ cup coconut flour
¼ cup pureed strawberries
½ cup egg whites
⅓ cup erythritol
1 large egg
½ stick of butter, melted
⅛ tsp. baking soda
½ tsp. baking powder
1 tsp. strawberry jello powder
½ tsp. vanilla
½ tsp. salt

Directions

1. Preheat your oven 350 F in advance. Combine the entire dry ingredients together in a large bowl; mixing the wet ingredients separately in another bowl.
2. Combine both the mixtures together until well incorporated & scoop the mixture into the lined cupcake tin. Bake in the preheated oven for 20 to 25 minutes; set aside and let completely cool.

KETO RED VELVET CUPCAKES

Prep Time: 12 minutes
Cooking Time: 15 minutes
Servings: 25

Nutritional Value (Estimated Amount Per Serving)

245 Calories
198 Calories from Fat
22g Total Fat
7.2g Saturated Fat
0.4g Trans Fat
3.4g Polyunsaturated Fat
10g Monounsaturated Fat
85mg Cholesterol
187mg Sodium
200mg Potassium
7g Total Carbohydrates
3g Dietary Fiber

1.3g Sugars
7.3g Protein

Ingredients

4 large eggs
2 ½ cups almond flour
½ cup granulated erythritol
8 tbsp. melted butter
2 tbsp. cocoa powder
3 tbsp. almond or coconut milk, unsweetened
¼ cup heavy cream
2 ½ tsp. baking powder
1 tsp. of liquid stevia
2 tsp. vanilla extract
Red food coloring as needed

Directions

1. Line a standard-sized cupcake pan with 12 cupcake liners and then preheat your oven to 325 F in advance.
2. Combine the entire dry ingredients together in a large bowl.
3. Melt the butter in a medium-sized microwave-safe bowl and then add the almond/coconut milk, heavy cream, vanilla extract, eggs & liquid stevia; mix well. Add in the food coloring until you get nice red color like consistency.
4. Add red liquid mixture to the dry mixture; mix well; but ensure that you don't over-mix.
5. Fill the cupcake cups approximately ¾ full with the prepared batter.
6. Bake in the preheated oven until a toothpick comes out clean, for 25 to 30 minutes. Let cool.
7. Once done, frost your cupcakes with the cream cheese icing & preferred garnishing ingredients. Serve & enjoy.

KETO MINI COFFEE CHOCOLATE CUPCAKES

Prep Time: 10 minutes
Cooking Time: 12 minutes
Servings: 30

Nutritional Value (Estimated Amount Per Serving)

213 Calories
37 Calories from Fat
4.2g Total Fat
0.6g Saturated Fat
0g Trans Fat
0.7g Polyunsaturated Fat
2.6g Monounsaturated Fat
0mg Cholesterol
11mg Sodium
171mg Potassium
40g Total Carbohydrates
8.2g Dietary Fiber
0.6g Sugars
5.3g Protein

Ingredients

1 tbsp. baking powder
2 tbsp. unsweetened cocoa powder
1 cup almond flour
2 large eggs
¼ cup Flaxseed Meal
1 tbsp. almond butter
2 tbsp. butter
¼ cup brewed coffee
4 tbsp. Erythritol
¼ cup almond milk
1 tbsp. olive oil
For Toppings:
100 g dark chocolate 85%, without added sugar
2 tbsp. brewed coffee
1 tbsp. Erythritol

Directions

1. Combine the entire ingredients for the cake in a large-sized mixing bowl using an electric mixer. Thoroughly blend until combined well. Lightly coat a cupcake

baking sheet with some of the coconut oil & pour the prepared cake mixture over the sheet.

2. Now, preheat your oven to 350 F in advance. Once done; bake in the preheated oven for 10 to 12 minutes.

3. In the meantime, prepare the frosting. Combine the chocolate with hot coffee & sweetener for a couple of minutes, until everything is melted & combined well.

4. Remove the cupcakes carefully from the sheet & frost them with the prepared coffee-chocolate mixture. Serve immediately & enjoy.

CARAMEL CUPCAKES WITH MILK CHOCOLATE FROSTING

Prep Time: 20 minutes
Cooking Time: 30 minutes
Servings: 12

Nutritional Value (Estimated Amount Per Serving)

264 Calories
196 Calories from Fat
22g Total Fat
8.1g Saturated Fat
0.4g Trans Fat
3g Polyunsaturated Fat
9.4g Monounsaturated Fat
60mg Cholesterol
242mg Sodium
199mg Potassium
3g Total Carbohydrates
2.5g Dietary Fiber
7.9g Sugars
7.4g Protein

Ingredients

2 cups almond flour
¼ tsp. of liquid stevia extract
1 recipe caramel sauce, sugar-free
¼ cup powdered egg whites or unflavored whey protein powder
2 large eggs
1/3 cup cashew or almond milk
2 tsp. baking powder
1 tsp. vanilla extract or caramel
¼ tsp. salt

For Milk Chocolate Frosting

4 to 6 tbsp. heavy whipping cream, at room temperature
½ cup softened butter
3 ounces chopped creamy milk chocolate
½ tsp. vanilla extract
2 cups swerve sweetener, powdered

Directions

1. Line a standard-sized muffin tin (preferably with 12 cavities) with paper liners and preheat your oven to 325 F.

2. Whisk the almond flour together with baking powder, whey protein & salt in a large bowl.

3. Add in the eggs, caramel sauce, vanilla extract or caramel & nut milk; continue to whisk until combined well.

4. Evenly divide the prepared batter among the muffin tin & bake until a tester comes out clean, for 25 to 30 minutes.

5. Remove & let completely cool in the pan.

For Frosting:

1. Now, melt the chocolate in a heatproof bowl placed over a pan of barely simmering water until completely smooth.

2. Beat the sweetener with butter in a large bowl until combined well. Add in the chocolate & continue to beat until well combined.

3. Add vanilla extract 4 and tbsp. of the whipping cream; continue to beat until completely smooth. Feel free to add more of whipping cream if the frosting is too thick until you get spreadable consistency.

4. Pipe or spread onto the cooled cupcakes

ALMOND FLOUR CUPCAKES

Prep Time: 15 minutes
Cooking Time: 25 minutes
Servings: 12

Nutritional Value (Estimated Amount Per Serving)

266 Calories
177 Calories from Fat
20g Total Fat
5.2g Saturated Fat
0g Trans Fat
3.8g Polyunsaturated Fat
9.6g Monounsaturated Fat
47mg Cholesterol
159mg Sodium
231mg Potassium
18g Total Carbohydrates
3.5g Dietary Fiber
13g Sugars
7.5g Protein

Ingredients

½ tsp. almond extract
3 cups blanched almond flour
¼ cup coconut oil, melted
3 large eggs, at room temperature
½ cup honey
2 tsp. vanilla extract
½ tsp. baking soda
1 tsp. lemon zest, fresh
½ tsp. salt

Directions

1. Line a standard-sized muffin pan (with 12 cups) with baking cups; set aside and then, preheat your oven to 325 F in advance.
2. Whisk the almond flour together with baking soda & salt in a large bowl; set aside.
3. Whisk the melted coconut oil together with eggs, honey, almond extract, vanilla extract & lemon zest in a medium bowl until combined well. Add wet ingredients into the bowl & continue to mix until combined well.
4. Evenly scoop or pour the prepared batter into the cupcake tins & bake until turn golden brown & a toothpick comes out clean, for 22 to 25 minutes. Let cool for 5 minutes and then remove to a wire rack to completely cool.
5. Frost the cooled cupcakes as desired. Serve and enjoy.

SUGAR FREE ITALIAN CREAM CUPCAKES

Prep Time: 20 minutes
Cooking Time: 20 minutes
Servings: 12

Nutritional Value (Estimated Amount Per Serving)

756 Calories
270 Calories from Fat
30g Total Fat
10g Saturated Fat
0.5g Trans Fat
2.8g Polyunsaturated Fat
14g Monounsaturated Fat
42mg Cholesterol
488mg Sodium
575mg Potassium
94g Total Carbohydrates
5.6g Dietary Fiber
7.5g Sugars
28g Protein

Ingredients

½ cup shredded, unsweetened coconut, toasted
¼ cup pecans, chopped
½ cup Greek yogurt
4 large eggs
½ tsp. vanilla extract
½ cup unrefined, softened pure, coconut oil
1 cup Quick Mix or DIY Local Blend or THM Baking Blend
½ tbsp. butter
¼ tsp. baking soda
½ cup Gentle Sweet
1 tsp. baking powder
¼ tsp. salt

For Cream Cheese Frosting:

> ½ cup Swerve Confectioners Sweetener or powdered xylitol
> ¼ cup Gentle Sweet
> ½ cup unsalted butter, softened (4 oz)
> 8 oz slightly softened cream cheese
> ½ tsp. vanilla extract

Directions

1. Line a standard-sized muffin pan with 12 cupcake liners and then preheat your oven to 350 F in advance.
2. Over moderate heat settings in a buttered, heavy bottom skillet; quickly toast the unsweetened coconut until turn brown, for a couple of minutes, stirring frequently to prevent burning.
3. Combine the softened coconut oil in a glass bowl, preferably large-sized and then add in the vanilla, yogurt and sweetener; beat well and then slowly add in the eggs & the wet ingredients; beat well.
4. Stir approximately 1/3 cup of the toasted coconut into wet ingredients and then add in the dry ingredients.
5. Sprinkle the baking blend over the wet ingredients and then sprinkle with baking powder, baking soda, nuts & salt on top; mix well until just mixed.
6. Fill the lined muffin cups approximately 2/3 full with the prepared batter.
7. Bake for 20 to 25 minutes. Set aside and let cool.

For Frosting

1. Whip the butter with softened cream cheese until smooth, for a minute or two.
2. Mix in the vanilla and then stir in the powdered sweetener; mix well until completely smooth & fluffy.
3. Frost the cupcakes with this frosting.
4. Refrigerate for a couple of minutes. Serve and enjoy.

KETO BLUEBERRY CUPCAKES

Prep Time: 15 minutes
Cooking Time: 25 minutes
Servings: 6

Nutritional Value (Estimated Amount Per Serving)

258 Calories
209 Calories from Fat
23g Total Fat
14g Saturated Fat
0.6g Trans Fat
1.3g Polyunsaturated Fat
6g Monounsaturated Fat
138mg Cholesterol
316mg Sodium
94mg Potassium
5.3g Total Carbohydrates
1.1g Dietary Fiber
7g Sugars
4.1g Protein

Ingredients

> ¼ cup coconut flour
> 3 large eggs
> ¼ cup erythritol or low carb sweetener
> 5 tbsp. blueberry blended mixture
> ¼ cup melted butter
> 1 tsp. vanilla extract
> ½ tsp. baking powder
> ¼ tsp. salt
> For Frosting:
> ¼ cup softened butter
> 4 oz softened cream cheese
> 1 tbsp. erythritol
> 5 tbsp. blueberry blended mixture
> ½ tsp. vanilla extract

Directions

1. Blitz the blueberries in a high power blender; set aside.
2. Blend the eggs together with butter, vanilla essence and erythritol.

3. Add in the baking powder, coconut flour & salt. Whisk for a minute or two, until completely smooth
4. Add in the blueberry mixture; combine well. Fill the cupcake cups approximately ¾ full with the prepared batter.
5. Bake until firm, for half an hour, at 400 F. Remove & let cool.

For The Frosting

1. Blend the cream cheese together with butter, vanilla and erythritol until completely smooth.
2. Add in the blueberry blend; continue to mix until combined well. Slather or pipe the mixture over the cupcakes.
3. Serve immediately & enjoy.

ROOT BEER FLOAT CUPCAKES

Prep Time: 15 minutes
Cooking Time: 25 minutes
Servings: 12

Nutritional Value (Estimated Amount Per Serving)

302 Calories
234 Calories from Fat
26g Total Fat
9g Saturated Fat
0.5g Trans Fat
3.8g Polyunsaturated Fat
12g Monounsaturated Fat
67mg Cholesterol
248mg Sodium
235mg Potassium
4g Total Carbohydrates
3.6g Dietary Fiber
4.8g Sugars
9.4g Protein

Ingredients

½ tsp. xanthan gum
2 2/3 cups almond flour
1/3 cup unflavored whey protein
2 tsp. baking powder
¼ tsp. Stevia Extract
5 tbsp. butter softened
¼ cup cocoa powder
2 large eggs
1/3 cup Swerve Sweetener
2 tsp. root beer extract
½ tsp. baking soda
1 cup Root Beer Honest Tea, sugar-free
¼ tsp. salt

For Frosting:

1/3 cup Swerve Sweetener, powdered
1 cup whipping cream
½ tsp. vanilla extract

Directions

1. Line a standard-sized muffin pan with paper liners and then preheat your oven to 325 F.
2. Whisk the almond flour together with whey protein, cocoa powder, xanthan gum, baking soda & salt in a medium-sized bowl.
3. Beat Swerve with butter in a large bowl for a minute or two, until completely creamy. Slowly beat in the eggs and then beat in the stevia extract and Root Beer extract.
4. Work in batches and beat in the almond flour mixture; alternating with root beer; scraping down the sides of your bowl & beaters, as required.
5. Evenly divide the prepared batter among the muffin cups & bake until a tester comes out clean, for 25 to 30 minutes.
6. Let completely cool in the pan.
7. For Frosting: Combine powdered Swerve together with vanilla extract & cream in large bowl. Continue to beat for a couple of minutes, until stiff peaks form; ensure that you don't overbeat the ingredients.
8. Spoon or pipe the mixture onto the cooled cupcakes.

KETOGENIC BAR RECIPES

GRANOLA BARS

Prep Time: 25 minutes
Cooking Time: 15 minutes
Servings: 12

Nutritional Value (Estimated Amount Per Serving)

186 Calories
152 Calories from Fat
17g Total Fat
5.9g Saturated Fat
0g Trans Fat
2.8g Polyunsaturated Fat
7.2g Monounsaturated Fat
16mg Cholesterol
204mg Sodium
195mg Potassium
6.1g Total Carbohydrates
3.5g Dietary Fiber
1.5g Sugars
5.4g Protein

Ingredients

1 cup raw almonds, chopped
4 tbsp. Monk-fruit sweetener
1 large egg
2 tbsp. almond butter
1 tbsp. coconut oil
¼ cup stevia sweetened chocolate chips
1 cup slivered almonds
¾ tsp. sea salt
1 cup tightly packed coconut flakes, unsweetened

Directions

1. Line a standard sized pan, preferably 8x8" with the parchment paper, leaving some hanging on the sides and then preheat your oven to 375 F in advance.

2. Place the coconut flakes, slivered almonds and chopped almonds on three separate baking sheets, preferably small-sized. Bake in the preheated oven until turn golden brown & toasted; set aside & let completely cool.

3. Now, whisk the egg together with monkfruit in a large bowl. Melt the coconut oil and almond butter in a small-sized microwave-safe bowl for half a minute, until smooth. Pour the mixture into the egg mixture; whisk until combined well.

4. Add in all the coconut, nuts & salt; give everything a good stir until combined well and then stir in the chocolate chips; pressing the mixture VERY firmly into the pan. Bake again for 12 to 15 more minutes, until the top is just set. Set the pan aside at room temperature and let cool completely. Slice; serve and enjoy.

KETO COCONUT BAR

Prep Time: 10 minutes
Cooking Time: 15 minutes
Servings: 24

Nutritional Value (Estimated Amount Per Serving)

119 Calories
95 Calories from Fat
11g Total Fat
9.2g Saturated Fat
0g Trans Fat
0.1g Polyunsaturated Fat
0.6g Monounsaturated Fat
0.3mg Cholesterol
17mg Sodium
70mg Potassium
6.3g Total Carbohydrates
1.9g Dietary Fiber
3.6g Sugars
1g Protein

Ingredients

- 1 oz chocolate minimum, sugar-free or dark, 85% cocoa solids
- 3 cups desiccated coconut unsweetened
- ½ cup sugar-free syrup
- 4 tbsp. coconut oil
- 1/3 cup coconut cream

Directions

1. Blend the entire ingredients together using an electric mixer or in a high power blender until moist & sticky.
2. Line a standard-sized pan, preferably 8x5" with the parchment paper & fill it with the prepared coconut mix; pressing down the mix using your hands until nice & firm. Using a large spatula; smooth the top & place in a fridge for several minutes. Remove & cut into desired pieces.
3. Now, melt the chocolate in a microwave.
4. Fill the melted chocolate into a large-sized plastic bag & pierce a hole using a needle. Drizzle the melted chocolate over the coconut bars.
5. Place the bars again into the fridge and let chill until firms up, for 10 more minutes.

KETO NUT BAR

Prep Time: 10 minutes
Cooking Time: 60 minutes
Servings: 6

Nutritional Value (Estimated Amount Per Serving)

271 Calories
189 Calories from Fat
21g Total Fat
5.4g Saturated Fat
0g Trans Fat
3.9g Polyunsaturated Fat
10g Monounsaturated Fat
0mg Cholesterol
167mg Sodium
247mg Potassium
7g Total Carbohydrates

3.8g Dietary Fiber
7.7g Sugars
6.1g Protein

Ingredients

- ½ tsp. vanilla essence
- 1 ¾ tbsp. almond butter or peanut butter
- 1/3 cup desiccated coconut
- 1 ¼ tbsp. coconut oil or butter
- ¼ cup Sukrin Gold Fiber Syrup
- ½ tbsp. chia seeds
- 1 ¼ cups Mixed seeds & nuts such as walnuts, almonds, sunflower seeds & pumpkin seeds
- ¼ tsp. salt

Directions

1. Line a square baking tin, preferably 20cm with the baking paper or grease it slightly.
2. Chop any larger nuts roughly or just leave them for a more crumbly bar. Now, combine the nuts with chia seeds, desiccated coconut & salt in a large bowl.
3. Add coconut butter or oil together with vanilla, fiber syrup and almond butter in a small microwave proof bowl.
4. Microwave until combines easily, for 30 seconds. Thoroughly stir to mix everything together evenly. Pour the melted mixture on top of the seeds and nuts; combine them thoroughly.
5. Pour the mixture into the prepared baking tin & push down firmly using the back of a measuring cup; spread the mixture evenly. Freeze for an hour and then cut into pieces; refrigerate until ready to serve. Enjoy.

KETO LEMON BAR

Prep Time: 15 minutes
Cooking Time: 45 minute
Servings: 8

Nutritional Value (Estimated Amount Per Serving)

290 Calories
231 Calories from Fat

26g Total Fat
8.8g Saturated Fat
0.5g Trans Fat
3.8g Polyunsaturated Fat
11g Monounsaturated Fat
100mg Cholesterol
135mg Sodium
253mg Potassium
7g Total Carbohydrates
4g Dietary Fiber
2g Sugars
8.1g Protein

Ingredients

1 ¾ cups almond flour
3 medium lemons
½ cup butter, melted
3 large eggs
1 cup erythritol, powdered

Directions

1. Combine butter together with ¼ cup of erythritol, a cup of almond flour & a pinch of salt; mix well. Press the mixture evenly into an 8×8" baking dish lined with parchment paper. Bake at 350 F for 20 minutes. Let cool for 8 to 10 minutes.
2. Zest one of the lemons in a large bowl and then juice the entire lemons; slowly add in the eggs followed by ¾ cup almond flour, ¾ cup erythritol & pinch of salt; mix everything together and prepare the filling.
3. Pour the prepared filling onto the crust & bake again for 20 to 25 more minutes. Serve with a sprinkle of erythritol & lemon slices on side.

PEANUT BUTTER CHOCOLATE BAR

Prep Time: 10 minutes
Cooking Time: 10 minutes
Servings: 8

Nutritional Value (Estimated Amount Per Serving)

289 Calories

221 Calories from Fat
25g Total Fat
8.6g Saturated Fat
0.2g Trans Fat
3.5g Polyunsaturated Fat
9.8g Monounsaturated Fat
15mg Cholesterol
123mg Sodium
175mg Potassium
13g Total Carbohydrates
3.4g Dietary Fiber
4.9g Sugars
7g Protein

Ingredients

For The Bars

2 oz butter
½ cup peanut butter
¾ cup almond flour
¼ cup Swerve Icing sugar style
½ tsp. vanilla

For The Topping

½ cup chocolate chips, sugar-free

Directions

1. Mix the entire bars ingredients together in a large bowl; mix well and then spread the mixture into a small-sized pan, preferably 6".
2. Heat the chocolate chips for 30 seconds in a microwave oven until melted & then stir. Spread the topping on top of the bars.
3. Refrigerate until the bars thicken up, for an hour or two. Serve and enjoy.

CHOCOLATE BAR

Prep Time: 10 minutes
Cooking Time: 10 minutes
Servings: 1

Nutritional Value (Estimated Amount Per Serving)

213 Calories
37 Calories from Fat

4.2g Total Fat
0.6g Saturated Fat
0g Trans Fat
0.7g Polyunsaturated Fat
2.6g Monounsaturated Fat
0mg Cholesterol
11mg Sodium
171mg Potassium
40g Total Carbohydrates
8.2g Dietary Fiber
0.6g Sugars
5.3g Protein

Ingredients

1 oz baker's chocolate, unsweetened
4 tbsp. unsalted butter
3 tbsp. powdered erythritol
1 tbsp. heavy cream
¼ tsp. vanilla extract
A pinch of salt

Directions

1. Heat an ounce of unsweetened baker's chocolate together with 4 tbsp. of butter in a microwave until completely melted, stir well.
2. Add in 3 tbsp of powdered erythritol & 1 tbsp of heavy cream; give everything a good stir.
3. Add in the vanilla & salt; stir well.
4. Pour the chocolate batter into chocolate mold and on top of the cracked sea salt.
5. Shake well until the chocolate spreads into the corners. Freeze & enjoy.

COCONUT CASHEW QUEST BARS

Prep Time: 5 minutes
Cooking Time: 5 minutes
Servings: 4

Nutritional Value (Estimated Amount Per Serving)

120 Calories
23 Calories from Fat

2.6g Total Fat
1.1g Saturated Fat
0g Trans Fat
0.3g Polyunsaturated Fat
1g Monounsaturated Fat
1.8mg Cholesterol
59mg Sodium
89mg Potassium
5g Total Carbohydrates
0.7g Dietary Fiber
8.5g Sugars
9.6g Protein

Ingredients

¼ cup flaked coconut, unsweetened
140 grams VitaFiber syrup
¼ cup lightly salted & roasted cashews, finely chopped
4 scoops unflavored whey protein
½ tsp. vanilla extract

Directions

1. Heat the VitaFiber syrup until it just begins to bubble in a microwave for 30 to 40 seconds.
2. Mix in the leftover ingredients; mix well.
3. Form the mixture into a rectangular shape.
4. Let cool in a refrigerator for a couple of hours. Evenly cut into four bars & individually wrap.

FATHEAD BLUEBERRY BARS

Prep Time: 30 minutes
Cooking Time: 30 minutes
Servings: 12

Nutritional Value (Estimated Amount Per Serving)

286 Calories
206 Calories from Fat
23g Total Fat
9g Saturated Fat
0.3g Trans Fat
2.8g Polyunsaturated Fat

9.4g Monounsaturated Fat
64mg Cholesterol
210mg Sodium
213mg Potassium
3g Total Carbohydrates
3.5g Dietary Fiber
6.6g Sugars
10g Protein

Ingredients

1 ¼ cup almond flour
1 tsp. vanilla
2 ounces cream cheese
1 tsp. cinnamon
2 tbsp. sour cream
1 ½ cup mozzarella
Zest of lemon
2 cups blueberries
1 beaten egg large
½ stick softened butter (ensure that it's not melted)
2 tsp. xantham
½ cup sweetener

Directions

1. Melt cream cheese together with mozzarella in a microwave safe dish; stir until completely smooth.
2. Cream butter together with vanilla, sweetener, almond flour, egg, sour cream and cinnamon in a separate bowl. Combine the cheese mixture into batter for a couple of minutes, until you get soft dough like consistency.
3. Feel free to add more of almond flour, if the dough seems to be quite sticky and continue to mix until you get cookie dough like consistency. Spoon the batter onto plastic wrap or parchment paper. Roll into ball; wrap & let refrigerate until ready to use.
4. Now, over medium low heat settings in a large sauce pan; cook the blueberries, mixing frequently. Bring the berries to a boil, when you can see enough of liquid, mixing frequently.

5. Stir in the xantham gum and decrease the heat settings to simmer until the sauce thickens and you get filling like consistency. Add in the lemon zest; stir well. Remove the pan from heat & set aside at room temperature.
6. Preheat your oven to 400 F in advance. Press approximately ¾ of the chilled dough into a greased pan, preferably 8x8" or 9x9" & bake for 10 minutes. Let cool until the sides recede, for 5 minutes.
7. Spoon the blueberry mixture into the crust & spread it evenly. Top with the leftover dough pieces. Bake again until golden brown & completely set, for 10 to 15 minutes more. Let completely cool and then cut into desired pieces

FROZEN STRAWBERRY CRUMBLE BARS

Prep Time: 15 minutes
Cooking Time: 45 minutes
Servings: 9

Nutritional Value (Estimated Amount Per Serving)

428 Calories
359 Calories from Fat
40g Total Fat
18g Saturated Fat
0.8g Trans Fat
4.3g Polyunsaturated Fat
15g Monounsaturated Fat
83mg Cholesterol
97mg Sodium
322mg Potassium
13g Total Carbohydrates
3.9g Dietary Fiber
7.3g Sugars
8.6g Protein

Ingredients

For The Bar Filling:

2 cup strawberries, fresh, clean & chopped into small chunks

¾ cup powdered sweetener, low-carb
2 cup heavy whipping cream
4 oz. soft cream cheese, full-fat
2 egg whites; whipped
2 tbsp. sweetener, low-carb

For The Crust And Topping:

3 tbsp. low-carb sweetener, powdered
2 cup almond 'meal'
3 tbsp. soft butter, at room temperature

Directions

1. Marinate the strawberries chunks in 2 tbsp. of sweetener for an hour.
2. Spray or grease a standard-sized cake pan, preferably 8x 8" and then preheat your oven to 350 F.
3. Mix the entire crust & topping ingredients together in a large bowl.
4. Press approximately 1 ½ cup of the mixture into the bottom of your prepared pan & bake until slightly golden brown, for 12 to 15 minutes. Remove & let cool at room temperature.
5. Whip the cream until soft peaks form and then slowly add in the sweetener and cream cheese; mix well.
6. Blend in the marinated strawberries; mix well and then fold in the whipped egg whites until incorporated well.
7. Spoon the filling over the crust & evenly smooth it out. Sprinkle with the leftover toppings. Using a plastic wrap; cover & let freeze for overnight.
8. Remove & slice into squares using a sharp knife.
9. Let rest for an hour. Serve and enjoy.

STRAWBERRY SWIRL CHEESECAKE BARS

Prep Time: 20 minutes
Cooking Time: 30 minutes
Servings: 30

Nutritional Value (Estimated Amount Per Serving)

55 Calories
28 Calories from Fat
3.2g Total Fat
1.6g Saturated Fat
0.1g Trans Fat
0.4g Polyunsaturated Fat
0.8g Monounsaturated Fat
19mg Cholesterol
48mg Sodium
35mg Potassium
5.7g Total Carbohydrates
0.3g Dietary Fiber
2.4g Sugars
1g Protein

Ingredients

1 pkg. frozen strawberries, thawed (10 oz.)
1 ¾ cups cinnamon graham cracker crumbs, finely crushed
1 tbsp. cornstarch
1/3 cup lemon juice, fresh
2 pkgs. cream cheese, softened (8 oz.)
1 can Eagle Brand® Sweetened Condensed Milk (14 oz.)
¼ cup butter, melted (4 tbsp.)
2 large eggs
1 tsp. vanilla extract

Directions

1. Lightly coat a 13x9" baking pan with the no-stick cooking spray and preheat your oven to 350 F in advance.
2. Add strawberries in a high power blender; blend on high settings until completely smooth. Transfer to a large saucepan and then add in the cornstarch. Cook & stir over moderate heat settings for a couple of

minutes, until thickened. Set aside and let cool.

3. Now, in small bowl; combine butter with graham cracker crumbs; press firmly into the bottom of your pan.

4. In a large bowl; beat the cream cheese for a minute or two, until fluffy. Slowly beat in the sweetened condensed milk and continue to beat until completely smooth. Add eggs followed by vanilla and lemon juice; mix well and then pour the mixture on top of the crust.

5. Using spoonfuls; drop the strawberry mixture over the batter. Gently swirl with a spatula or knife.

6. Bake in the preheated oven until the middle is just set, for 25 to 30 minutes. Let completely cool & then chill in a refrigerator. Once done; cut into bars. Serve and enjoy.

ALMOND JOY BARS

Prep Time: 15 minutes
Cooking Time: 25 minutes
Servings: 16

Nutritional Value (Estimated Amount Per Serving)

294 Calories
239 Calories from Fat
27g Total Fat
16g Saturated Fat
0.1g Trans Fat
1.9g Polyunsaturated Fat
6.9g Monounsaturated Fat
5.4mg Cholesterol
104mg Sodium
152mg Potassium
12g Total Carbohydrates
3.4g Dietary Fiber
6.8g Sugars
3.5g Protein

Ingredients

For Crust:

   ½ tsp baking soda

   1 ½ cups almond flour
   ¼ cup coconut oil
   2 tbsp classic monk fruit sweetener
   ¼ cup plus 1 tbsp. coconut flour
   1/8 tsp salt

For Chocolate:

   100g cocoa butter
   5 tbsp. heavy whipping cream
   5 tbsp. unsweetened cocoa powder
   ¼ cup classic monk fruit sweetener

For Coconut:

   1/3 cup classic monk fruit sweetener
   2 cups coconut, shredded
   ½ tsp. pure vanilla extract
   1/3 cup coconut oil, melted

For Topping:

   16 almonds, raw

Directions

For The Crust:

1. Line a standard-sized baking pan, preferably 8×8" with the parchment paper and then preheat your oven to 325 F in advance.

2. Pulse the entire crust ingredients together in food processor for a minute or two, until combined well.

3. Transfer the prepared mixture into the baking pan & press the crust into even layer using fingers.

4. Bake in the preheated oven for 15 to 20 minutes, until the crust turn golden brown.

5. Set aside to cool slightly.

For The Coconut Layer:

1. In the meantime, pulse the entire coconut ingredients together in a food processor for a minute or two, until combined well.

2. Once the crust has cooled off slightly, press the coconut mixture into even layer over the crust, using fingers.

For The Chocolate Layer:

1. Add cocoa powder together with cocoa butter, monk fruit sweetener & heavy whipping cream to a small glass bowl.

2. Melt the ingredients together over medium low heat on stovetop (using the double boiler method) until the chocolate is completely smooth, whisk the mixture frequently.
3. Pour the chocolate mixture on top of coconut layer & using a large spatula smooth into even layer.
4. Transfer the pan to a freezer and let chill for 30 to 40 minutes, until the chocolate hardens.
5. Remove the pan from freezer & evenly cut the bars into 16 pieces.

For The Almonds:

1. Over medium low heat settings in a small pan; heat the almonds for a couple of minutes, until turn golden.
2. Remove the almonds from heat & carefully place individual almonds over the chocolate layer using a tongs, pressing down gently until the chocolate just melts & acts as glue. Whisk the egg yolks together with lemon zest, lemon juice, liquid stevia & vanilla in a medium bowl.
3. Whisk in the heavy cream & evenly divide the mixture between small jars or ramekins.
4. Place a rack in the bottom of your slow cooker & place the jars on the rack. Add water enough to reach halfway up the sides of your jars.
5. Cover & cook for 3 hours on low-heat settings.
6. Remove the jars; set aside & let cool at room temperature until easy to handle and then let chill in a refrigerator for 2 to 3 hours. Top with the whipped cream; serve & enjoy.

MOCK SNICKERS BAR

Prep Time: 20 minutes
Cooking Time: 30 minutes
Servings: 16

Nutritional Value (Estimated Amount Per Serving)

226 Calories
188 Calories from Fat
21g Total Fat
8.9g Saturated Fat
0.4g Trans Fat
2.5g Polyunsaturated Fat
7.8g Monounsaturated Fat
28mg Cholesterol
102mg Sodium
161mg Potassium
3g Total Carbohydrates
2.4g Dietary Fiber
1.6g Sugars
4.7g Protein

Ingredients

For Shortbread Crust:

> *¼ cup butter, chilled*
> *1 ¼ cups almond flour*
> *¼ cup granulated stevia*
> *15 drops of liquid stevia*
> *½ tsp. xanthan gum*

For Chocolate Topping:

> *2 ½ ounces chocolate, unsweetened*
> *6 tbsp. butter*
> *15 drops of liquid stevia*
> *2 tbsp. powdered Stevia*
> *½ tsp. vanilla extract*
> *2 tbsp. cocoa powder, unsweetened*

For Peanut Butter Caramel Filling:

> *½ cup smooth peanut butter*
> *½ cup granulated Stevia*
> *1 tsp. vanilla extract*
> *½ cup heavy whipping cream*

Directions

For Shortbread Crust

1. Preheat your oven to 350 F in advance.
2. Combine the almond flour together with stevia, butter, xanthan gum & liquid sweetener in a food processor, until combined well and you get fine crumby crust like consistency.
3. Evenly press the mixture into the bottom of a standard-sized baking pan, preferably 8"
4. Bake in the preheated oven until turn golden, for 12 to 15 minutes
5. Set aside & let cool

For Peanut Butter Caramel Filling:

1. Over medium-high heat settings in a small saucepan; combine stevia with 1 tsp. of water.
2. Give them a good stir for a couple of minutes, until the stevia is completely dissolved & the mixture starts to bubble.
3. Remove from heat & stir in the cream
4. Place the pan again on the heat & let boil for a minute more.
5. Stir in the vanilla extract and peanut butter until completely smooth
6. Pour the mixture on top of the cooled shortbread crust & evenly spread. Let completely cool.

For Chocolate Topping:

1. Over low heat settings in a small saucepan; melt the chocolate, butter & stevia; stirring occasionally until smoothed & glossy
2. Add in the cocoa powder; give everything a good stir until no lumps remain.
3. Add in the vanilla extract and liquid sweetener; stir again.
4. Pour the melted chocolate on top of the cooled peanut butter filling.
5. Let sit for an hour at room temp then let chill in a fridge until hardens.

KETO PUDDING RECIPES

STRAWBERRY MATCHA CHIA PUDDING

Prep Time: 4 hours & 5 minutes
Cooking Time: 5 minutes
Servings: 2

Nutritional Value (Estimated Amount Per Serving)

490 Calories
376 Calories from Fat
42g Total Fat
33g Saturated Fat
0g Trans Fat
4.7g Polyunsaturated Fat
2g Monounsaturated Fat
0mg Cholesterol
26mg Sodium
479mg Potassium
5g Total Carbohydrates
6.5g Dietary Fiber
18g Sugars
6.6g Protein

Ingredients

2 strawberries, diced small
½ tsp. matcha powder
1 ½ tbsp. chia seeds
¾ cup coconut milk
Raw honey or stevia to taste

Directions

1. Place coconut milk together with chia seeds, matcha powder & sweeteners into a large cup, preferably with a lid. Seal & shake for a few seconds.
2. Pour the mixture into a large glass & place in a fridge; let chill for a couple of hours.
3. Add the diced strawberries into the prepared pudding; mix well; serve topped with more of diced strawberries & enjoy.

KETO CHOCOLATE AVOCADO PUDDING

Prep Time: 5 minutes
Cooking Time: 5 minutes
Servings: 1

Nutritional Value (Estimated Amount Per Serving)

234 Calories
61 Calories from Fat
6.8g Total Fat
4.1g Saturated Fat
0g Trans Fat
0.3g Polyunsaturated Fat
1.9g Monounsaturated Fat
16mg Cholesterol
204mg Sodium
72mg Potassium
4g Total Carbohydrates
2.4g Dietary Fiber
0.1g Sugars
3.5g Protein

Ingredients

1 medium avocado, pit removed
¼ cup unsweetened cocoa powder
10 drops of liquid stevia
1 tsp. Himalayan pink salt
½ tsp. vanilla extract

Directions

1. Place the avocado in a large-sized mixing bowl.
2. Add in the cocoa powder, vanilla extract and stevia. Using a large fork; mix

everything together until you get pudding like consistency.

3. Top the recipe with a pinch of Himalayan pink sea salt. Serve & enjoy.

KETO RICE PUDDING

Prep Time: 5 minutes
Cooking Time: 20 minutes
Servings: 4

Nutritional Value (Estimated Amount Per Serving)

435 Calories
216 Calories from Fat
24g Total Fat
15g Saturated Fat
0.8g Trans Fat
1.3g Polyunsaturated Fat
6.1g Monounsaturated Fat
94mg Cholesterol
116mg Sodium
439mg Potassium
45g Total Carbohydrates
6.5g Dietary Fiber
3.2g Sugars
10g Protein

Ingredients

1 ½ cup konjac rice strained
1 bean vanilla seeds
2 cup heavy cream
1/3 cup erythritol or any low-carb sweetener
1 large egg
3 oz. dried tart cherries, instead of raisins
1 stick cinnamon
1 piece star anise
3 seeds cardamom, optional
1 tbsp. butter
¼ tsp. salt

Directions

1. Prepare the konjac rice as per the instructions mentioned on the package.

2. Combine the prepared konjac rice together with 1 ½ cup of heavy cream, vanilla seeds, sweetener, spices & salt over medium heat settings in a large saucepan.

3. Cook until somewhat dense, for 15 to 20 minutes.

4. Beat the egg & then stir it with the leftover heavy cream. At this point; feel free to add a few dried tart cherries.

5. Cook for 2 more minutes, stirring every now and then.

6. Remove from heat & stir in the butter.

7. Evenly divide the Keto Rice Pudding among 4 cups. Let completely cool in the fridge for overnight. Serve; sprinkled with the cinnamon powder and enjoy.

ESPRESSO CHOCOLATE PUDDING

Prep Time: 15 minutes
Cooking Time: 5 minutes
Servings: 4

Nutritional Value (Estimated Amount Per Serving)

443 Calories
299 Calories from Fat
33g Total Fat
21g Saturated Fat
1.1g Trans Fat
1.4g Polyunsaturated Fat
8.1g Monounsaturated Fat
101mg Cholesterol
25mg Sodium
94mg Potassium
4g Total Carbohydrates
2g Dietary Fiber
28g Sugars
4.5g Protein

Ingredients

½ cup sugar substitute
1 ½ cups heavy whipping cream
½ tsp. xanthan gum

1 oz. shot espresso
½ cup unsweetened cocoa

Directions

1. Heat up the heavy cream very slowly in a small-sized saucepan; while whisking, add in the sugar substitute, cocoa and espresso.
2. Once the sugar and cocoa has mixed in, add in the xanthan gum & bring everything together to a low simmer.
3. Continue to cook until it becomes thick; remove from heat & place into the bowls or ramekins & let chill for an hour.

RASPBERRY ALMOND CHIA PUDDING

Prep Time: 5 minutes
Cooking Time: 5 minutes
Servings: 2

Nutritional Value (Estimated Amount Per Serving)

233 Calories
89 Calories from Fat
9.9g Total Fat
2.3g Saturated Fat
0g Trans Fat
3.9g Polyunsaturated Fat
3.2g Monounsaturated Fat
12mg Cholesterol
91mg Sodium
424mg Potassium
17g Total Carbohydrates
7.5g Dietary Fiber
1.7g Sugars
21g Protein

Ingredients

2 tbsp. almonds, sliced
1 cup nut milk, unsweetened (such as coconut or almond)
2 tbsp. Chia Seeds plus ½ tbsp. more for a thicker pudding
A scoop of Vanilla protein powder
½ cup raspberries

Optional Ingredients:

Liquid stevia to taste
¼ tsp. almond extract

Directions

1. Evenly divide the ingredients between two small-sized containers (preferably with tight fitting lids).
2. Cover the containers with the lids & seal them tightly.
3. Vigorously shake until the ingredients are evenly mixed.
4. Let sit in a refrigerator for 5 hours. Serve and enjoy.

KETO CHIA PUDDING WITH ALMOND AND CINNAMON

Prep Time: 5 minutes
Cooking Time: 5minutes
Servings: 2

Nutritional Value (Estimated Amount Per Serving)

169 Calories
122 Calories from Fat
14g Total Fat
1.1g Saturated Fat
0g Trans Fat
5.3g Polyunsaturated Fat
6.1g Monounsaturated Fat
0mg Cholesterol
4mg Sodium
186mg Potassium
3g Total Carbohydrates
6.4g Dietary Fiber
0.8g Sugars
5.8g Protein

Ingredients

¼ tsp. of liquid stevia
2 tbsp. chia seeds
½ tsp. ground cinnamon
2 tbsp. almond butter
¾ cup almond milk, unsweetened

Directions

1. Add the entire ingredients (except the chia seeds) together into a large bowl.
2. Whisk the mixture for a couple of minutes, until the almond butter is completely dissolved.
3. Add in the chia seeds & mix well
4. Refrigerate for an hour and then give everything a good stir
5. Refrigerate for 2 more hours or for overnight
6. Feel free to add more of water or almond milk, if the mixture appears to be too thick
7. Serve chilled & enjoy.

KETO BREAD PUDDING

Prep Time: 5 minutes
Cooking Time: 5minutes
Servings: 5

Nutritional Value (Estimated Amount Per Serving)

348 Calories
182 Calories from Fat
20g Total Fat
11g Saturated Fat
0.2g Trans Fat
1.8g Polyunsaturated Fat
6.2g Monounsaturated Fat
148mg Cholesterol
229mg Sodium
124mg Potassium
7g Total Carbohydrates
2.2g Dietary Fiber
21g Sugars
7.2g Protein

Ingredients

4 tbsp unsalted butter
6 slices cinnamon bread; cut into cubes
1½ cups almond milk, unsweetened
30 g mini chocolate chips, low-carb
¼ cup sweetener, low-carb
3 large eggs

Directions

1. Preheat your oven to 375 F in advance.
2. Place the bread cubes in a large bowl.
3. Add milk in a medium-sized saucepan; bring it to a boil over moderate heat settings. Once boiling; decrease the heat settings & then add in the butter. Give it a good stir for a couple of minutes, until the butter is completely melted. Pour the prepared milk mixture on top of the bread; set aside for 10 minutes and let the bread to soak the milk.
4. Mix eggs with sweetener in a separate bowl.
5. Pour the egg mixture over the bread, and add the chocolate chips.
6. Pour everything into a baking dish (preferably greased with some butter); pushing down the bread. Bake until the egg mixture has completely set, for half an hour. Let cool for 5 minutes; serve & enjoy.

LOW CARB STICKY TOFFEE PUDDING

Prep Time: 15 minutes
Cooking Time: 20 minutes
Servings: 2

Nutritional Value (Estimated Amount Per Serving)

71 Calories
9.2 Calories from Fat
1g Total Fat
0.6g Saturated Fat
0g Trans Fat
0.1g Polyunsaturated Fat
0.3g Monounsaturated Fat
3.4mg Cholesterol
104mg Sodium
399mg Potassium
6g Total Carbohydrates
2.3g Dietary Fiber
9.5g Sugars
4.3g Protein

Ingredients

1 egg separated
½ cup almond flour
2 tbsp. heavy cream
½ tsp. baking powder
1 tbsp. unsalted butter, melted & cooled
2 tsp. sweetener (such as granular Swerve or xylitol)

For The Sauce:

2 tbsp. low-carb sweetener
1 tbsp. unsalted butter
¼ cup water
A pinch of thickener, low-carb (optional)

Directions

1. Preheat your oven to 350 F in advance.
2. For The Cake: Mix the egg yolk together with heavy cream, melted butter, sweetener and baking powder. Add in the almond flour; give everything a good stir until a thick paste like consistency is achieved.
3. Whisk the egg white for a couple of minutes, until soft peaks form and then carefully fold it into the almond mixture.
4. Fill the pudding cups with the prepared mixture. Place on a large-sized baking tray & bake in the preheated oven until the middle is cooked, for 10 to 12 minutes. Let cool for a couple of minutes and then turn them out on a cooling rack to completely cool.
5. For The Sauce: Over moderate heat settings in a small saucepan; add butter together with sweetener & water; bring it to a boil & continue to cook for 3 to 5 minutes. Keep an eye on everything; don't let it burn. Add a pinch of thickener & continue to whisk for a couple of minutes, until thickened.
6. Arrange the almond cakes on individual serving plates and then pour the warm sauce on top of them.

BLUEBERRY CHIA PUDDING

Prep Time: 5 minutes
Cooking Time: 1 minutes
Servings: 1

Nutritional Value (Estimated Amount Per Serving)

406 Calories
300 Calories from Fat
33g Total Fat
15g Saturated Fat
0.8g Trans Fat
9.7g Polyunsaturated Fat
6.7g Monounsaturated Fat
67mg Cholesterol
23mg Sodium
241mg Potassium
3g Total Carbohydrates
13g Dietary Fiber
5.5g Sugars
8.2g Protein

Ingredients

¼ cup blueberries or strawberries or raspberries, fresh or frozen.
3 tbsp. chia seeds
¼ cup almond milk, unsweetened
2 tsp. erythritol or 3-6 drops of liquid stevia
¼ cup coconut milk or heavy cream

Directions

1. Place the entire ingredients together in a small jar or bowl; mix well.
2. Place in a fridge and let chill for overnight.
3. When ready to eat; mix well; serve & enjoy.

KETO BANANA PUDDING

Prep Time: 15 minutes
Cooking Time: 20 minutes
Servings: 12

Nutritional Value (Estimated Amount Per Serving)

228 Calories
100 Calories from Fat
11g Total Fat
1g Saturated Fat
0.1g Trans Fat
2.4g Polyunsaturated Fat
7.1g Monounsaturated Fat
0mg Cholesterol
252mg Sodium
550mg Potassium
3g Total Carbohydrates
5.4g Dietary Fiber
22g Sugars
3.3g Protein

Ingredients

For The Cookie Layer:

> *1 large egg*
> *2 tbsp/ softened butter*
> *1 tsp baking powder*
> *½ cup super fine almond flour*
> *1 tsp vanilla extract*
> *¼ cup erythritol*

For The Pudding Layer:

> *6 egg yolks*
> *½ cup erythritol*
> *2 tsp vanilla extract*
> *1 cup unsweetened almond or coconut milk*
> *2 cups heavy whipping cream*
> *1 banana, medium, sliced thinly*

For The Whipped Cream Layer:

> *¼ cup erythritol or to taste*
> *1 tsp vanilla extract*
> *½ cup heavy whipping cream*
> *¼ tsp Xanthan Gum*

Directions

1. Line a large-sized baking sheet with the parchment paper and then preheat your oven to 350 F in advance.
2. Using an electric mixer; combine butter together with egg & vanilla in a large bowl then, add in the Almond flour, Erythritol & baking powder; mix well.
3. Once the mixture is combined well, spread it into an even layer on the baking sheet.
4. Bake until turn golden brown, for 12 to 15 minutes. Remove & set aside at room temperature to cool.
5. Meanwhile, start preparing the pudding. Add egg yolks to a medium-sized bowl; set aside. Add the almond milk together with heavy cream, erythritol and vanilla to a heavy-bottomed saucepan.
6. Heat the milk-cream mixture over medium heat settings until the cream begins to steam, stirring frequently. Remove from the heat & slowly whisk 1 ½ cups of warm cream in the yolks until smooth & uniform.
7. Slowly whisk this egg yolk-cream mixture into the leftover cream again
8. Cook over medium-low heat settings; continue to stir and scrape down the sides & bottom of your pan using a rubber spatula until the mixture thickens.
9. Remove the pan from heat; set aside & let cool slightly.
10. Cut the cookies roughly into 1" cubes.
11. Add ½ cup of the pudding to the bottom of an 8x8", 2-quarts dish & spread to cover the bottom. Now, use half of the cookies and form an even layer over the pudding; adding a layer using half of the sliced bananas and then half of the leftover pudding.
12. Cover the dish loosely & place it inside a fridge; let chill for an hour or two, until completely cool
13. Once done, prepare the whipped cream. Whip the cream together with erythritol, vanilla and xanthan gum using an electric mixer in a medium bowl for a couple of

minutes, until stiff peaks form. Spread this prepared whipped cream on top of the banana pudding; serve and enjoy

TAPIOCA PUDDING

Prep Time: 2 minutes
Cooking Time: 10 minutes
Servings: 4

Nutritional Value (Estimated Amount Per Serving)

526 Calories
269 Calories from Fat
30g Total Fat
7.9g Saturated Fat
0g Trans Fat
3.6g Polyunsaturated Fat
17g Monounsaturated Fat
16mg Cholesterol
189mg Sodium
581mg Potassium
5g Total Carbohydrates
5.9g Dietary Fiber
8.6g Sugars
11g Protein

Ingredients

½ cup almond milk, unsweetened
6 egg yolks, large
1 tsp vanilla
¼ cup melted coconut oil or butter
1 package Miracle Rice
¼ cup Swerve or erythritol
Cinnamon to taste

Directions

1. Whisk almond milk together with egg yolks, extract and natural sweetener in medium-sized metal bowl until blended well.
2. Gradually mix in the melted butter and ensure that the eggs don't cook unevenly.
3. Place the bowl on top of the saucepan with simmering water.
4. Continue to whisk the mixture until thickened.
5. Remove & stir in the Miracle Rice. The last step is to add the cinnamon to taste.
6. Serve as it is or chilled.

KETOGENIC ICE CREAM RECIPES

CHOCOLATE COCONUT KETO ICE CREAM

Prep Time: 15 minutes
Cooking Time: 30 minutes
Servings: 2

Nutritional Value (Estimated Amount Per Serving)

146 Calories
101 Calories from Fat
11g Total Fat
1.4g Saturated Fat
0g Trans Fat
1.2g Polyunsaturated Fat
6.7g Monounsaturated Fat
0mg Cholesterol
72mg Sodium
345mg Potassium
4g Total Carbohydrates
6.1g Dietary Fiber
0.6g Sugars
2.8g Protein

Ingredients

13 ounces coconut cream; frozen into ice cubes
1 avocado, ripe
A pinch of salt
1 to 3 Tbsp. cocoa powder
Sweetener to taste (such as liquid stevia)

Directions

1. Add the entire ingredients together into a food processor or high-power blender; blitz on high settings until smooth & creamy; scrapping down the sides, as required. Feel free to add a tablespoon of water or more until you get your desired consistency.
2. Taste and adjust the flavors of your ice cream or just add more of sweetener, if required. Evenly divide the mixture into two bowls and let chill in a refrigerator until ready to eat.

KETO MOCHA ICE CREAM

Prep Time: 15 minutes
Cooking Time: 30 minutes
Servings: 2

Nutritional Value (Estimated Amount Per Serving)

356 Calories
318 Calories from Fat
35g Total Fat
28g Saturated Fat
0.4g Trans Fat
0.7g Polyunsaturated Fat
3.7g Monounsaturated Fat
34mg Cholesterol
33mg Sodium
330mg Potassium
7g Total Carbohydrates
1g Dietary Fiber
0.9g Sugars
4.3g Protein

Ingredients

¼ cup heavy whipping cream
15 drops liquid Stevia
1 cup coconut milk (directly from the carton)
2 tbsp. erythritol
1 tbsp. instant coffee
2 tbsp. cocoa powder, unsweetened
¼ tsp. xanthan gum

Directions

1. Add the entire ingredients (don't add the xanthan gum) into the container of your blender; blend on high settings until completely smooth & creamy.

2. While blending; slowly add in the xanthan gum and continue to blend until thick.
3. Add the mixture to your ice cream machine & follow the instructions provided by the manufacturer.

LOW CARB BLUEBERRY BUTTERMILK ICE CREAM

Prep Time: 15 minutes
Cooking Time: 30 minutes
Servings: 2

Nutritional Value (Estimated Amount Per Serving)

609 Calories
245 Calories from Fat
27g Total Fat
4.2g Saturated Fat
0g Trans Fat
3.1g Polyunsaturated Fat
17g Monounsaturated Fat
25mg Cholesterol
617mg Sodium
343mg Potassium
5g Total Carbohydrates
1.2g Dietary Fiber
2.1g Sugars
15g Protein

Ingredients

2 tbsp. lemon juice
1/8 tsp. stevia glycerite
¼ cup erythritol
½ pound blueberries, washed & cleaned
1/8 tsp. almond extract
A pinch of freshly ground nutmeg
1/8 tsp. cinnamon
¼ tsp. vanilla extract
1 tbsp. water

For Blueberry-Buttermilk Ice Cream Base:

1 ½ cups heavy cream
½ tsp. stevia glycerite
1/3 cup erythritol
2 tbsp. vanilla flavored vodka

1 1/8 cups buttermilk
1 tsp. balsamic vinegar reduction
¼ tsp. salt

`Directions

1. For the Blueberry Puree:
2. Put the blueberries with two tablespoons lemon juice, 1 tablespoon water, nutmeg, cinnamon & ¼ cup of erythritol in a small-sized sauce pan. Cover & cook over medium to low heat settings until it starts to simmer. Once done; immediately decrease the heat settings to low & let simmer for 10 more minutes, covered.
3. Transfer the cooked blueberries to a high-power blender & blend on low speed until pureed. Transfer the pureed blueberry into the sauce pan again & let simmer for 20 to 30 more minutes, uncovered, stirring frequently. Remove from the heat and add the almond extract, stevia glycerite & vanilla. Give everything a good stir & let completely cool.

For Balsamic Vinegar Reduction:

1. Over moderate heat settings in a small-sized sauce pan; bring ¼ cup of the balsamic vinegar to simmer for a couple of minutes, until decreased by half. Set aside at room temperature and let cool. Use 1 teaspoon in the recipe; reserving the leftover for more ice cream.

For Blueberry Buttermilk Ice Cream Base:

1. Add the blueberry puree in the carafe of a blender & add in the entire ice cream base ingredients. Blend on low settings until completely pureed & mixed; then blend on high settings for a minute.

For Blueberry Buttermilk Ice Cream:

1. Simply follow the manufacturer's directions for freezing. Cover & place in the freezer. When ready to serve; let sit on the counter for a couple of minutes. Enjoy.

STRAWBERRY ICE CREAM

Prep Time: 10 minutes
Cooking Time: 15 minute
Servings: 5

Nutritional Value (Estimated Amount Per Serving)

369 Calories
305 Calories from Fat
34g Total Fat
30g Saturated Fat
0g Trans Fat
0.4g Polyunsaturated Fat
1.5g Monounsaturated Fat
0mg Cholesterol
23mg Sodium
509mg Potassium
5g Total Carbohydrates
2.3g Dietary Fiber
9.8g Sugars
3.7g Protein

Ingredients

16 oz strawberries, frozen
½ to ¾ cup equivalent sweetener (such as Swerve)
2 cans coconut milk (13.5 oz each)
½ cup fresh strawberries, chopped, optional

Directions

2. Combine the entire ingredients (don't add the optional strawberries) in a high-power blender & blend on high settings until completely smooth.
3. Fill your ice cream maker with the prepared mixture & process as per the directions provided by the manufacturer.
4. Just before the ice cream is done; add in the fresh strawberries and mix.
5. Serve immediately & enjoy. Or let freeze until ready to eat.

STRAWBERRY SWIRL ICE CREAM

Prep Time: 15 minutes
Cooking Time: 25 minutes
Servings: 6

Nutritional Value (Estimated Amount Per Serving)

182 Calories
150 Calories from Fat
17g Total Fat
10g Saturated Fat
0.5g Trans Fat
1g Polyunsaturated Fat
4.6g Monounsaturated Fat
137mg Cholesterol
22mg Sodium
92mg Potassium
4.8g Total Carbohydrates
0.6g Dietary Fiber
2.7g Sugars
2.7g Protein

Ingredients

3 egg yolks, large
1/3 cup erythritol
1 cup heavy whipping cream
1/8 tsp. xanthan gum
1 cup strawberries
½ tsp. vanilla extract
1 tbsp. vodka

Directions

1. Over moderate heat settings in a large pot; heat up the heavy cream. Add in approximately 1/3 cup of the erythritol; stir until completely dissolved; don't bring the cream to a boil; ensure that it just simmers gently.
2. Separate three egg yolks from whites and add them to a large-sized mixing bowl. Using an electric mixer; beat them until almost doubled in size (tempering the eggs and ensure that they don't scramble).

3. While beating; add in a couple tablespoons of the hot cream mixture to the eggs.
4. Continue to perform this step for a couple of more times, until the egg mixture is somewhat warm and then gradually add in the remaining cream mixture; continue to beat. Add in some of the vanilla extract & mix well.
5. Add in a tbsp. of the vodka & 1/8 tsp. of the xanthan gum.
6. Place in the bowl and then transfer into the freezer; let chill for a couple of hours, stirring every now and then.
7. When the ice cream is chilled & thick; add in the strawberries. Wash & hull a cup of the strawberries; puree for a second or two.
8. Add the strawberry mixture to the chilled cream. Mix but ensure that you don't over mix them.
9. Let chill for overnight. Serve and enjoy.

VANILLA KETO ICE CREAM

Prep Time: 10 minutes
Cooking Time: 10 minutes
Servings: 4

Nutritional Value (Estimated Amount Per Serving)

435 Calories
402 Calories from Fat
45g Total Fat
28g Saturated Fat
1.5g Trans Fat
2.1g Polyunsaturated Fat
12g Monounsaturated Fat
204mg Cholesterol
102mg Sodium
125mg Potassium
3.9g Total Carbohydrates
0g Dietary Fiber
3.9g Sugars
4.4g Protein

Ingredients

4 cups heavy whipping cream
3 large egg yolks

½ to 1 cup zero-sugar sweetener
4 tsp. beef gelatin
1 whole vanilla bean scraped
2 tbsp. pure vanilla extract
¼ tsp. sea salt

Directions

1. Freeze the bowl of your ice cream maker into the freezer for overnight.
2. Add the entire ingredients into a saucepan, preferably medium-sized; whisk well.
3. Now, over moderate heat settings in a large saucepan. Cook the mixture until it begins to steam, whisking consistently (ensure that you don't bring it to a boil). Remove from heat & let the mixture to cool a bit then transfer it to a large-sized sealable container. Refrigerate until completely chilled, for a couple of hours.
4. Give your ice cream base a good stir & pour the mixture into the ice cream maker. Turn it on & churn until creamy and very thick. Serve immediately and enjoy.

KETO COFFEE ICE CREAM

Prep Time: 10 minutes
Cooking Time: 15 minutes
Servings: 2

Nutritional Value (Estimated Amount Per Serving)

250 Calories
189 Calories from Fat
21g Total Fat
2.9g Saturated Fat
0g Trans Fat
2.5g Polyunsaturated Fat
13g Monounsaturated Fat
0mg Cholesterol
11mg Sodium
696mg Potassium
5g Total Carbohydrates
9.2g Dietary Fiber
3.4g Sugars
2.7g Protein

Ingredients

2 avocados, ripe, diced roughly & frozen

1 tbsp. Brain octane oil or water, if required

13 oz. coconut cream ice cubes

2 to 4 tbsp. Monkfruit sweetener or to taste

1 double shot of Bulletproof Coffee Espresso

1 to 2 tsp. pure vanilla extract

High-quality chocolate chips or whole coffee beans, for garnish

Directions

1. Remove the avocados & coconut cubes from freezer & let slightly thaw for 5 to 10 minutes at room temperature.
2. Add the entire ingredients into a food processor or high-power blender; blitz on high settings until smooth & creamy; scrapping down the sides of your bowl, as required & blend again a couple of times. If the mixture is too thick then, slowly add 1 tbsp of oil or water to the mix and continue to blend until smooth.
3. Taste and adjust the amount of sweetness, if required.
4. When done, scoop into two large bowls & enjoy.

LOW CARB PECAN PRALINE ICE CREAM

Prep Time: 10 minutes
Cooking Time: 15 minutes
Servings: 6

Nutritional Value (Estimated Amount Per Serving)

71 Calories

9.2 Calories from Fat

1g Total Fat

0.6g Saturated Fat

0g Trans Fat

0.1g Polyunsaturated Fat

0.3g Monounsaturated Fat

3.4mg Cholesterol

104mg Sodium

399mg Potassium

4g Total Carbohydrates

2.3g Dietary Fiber

9.5g Sugars

4.3g Protein

Ingredients

2 cups Silk protein plus fiber almond milk or unsweetened almond milk

¼ tsp caramel flavored extract

5 egg yolks

½ cup heavy whipping cream

3 Tbsp granulated sugar substitute

¼ tsp xanthan gum

1 tsp butter flavored extract

¼ cup chopped pecans

1 tsp butter

½ tsp. kosher salt

Directions

1. In a medium-sized bowl; combine heavy whipping cream with almond milk.
2. Microwave for 2 minutes on high-power.
3. Stir in the butter extract, sugar substitute, egg yolks, caramel extract, xanthan gum and kosher salt until completely smooth, for a couple of minutes.
4. Microwave for 30 seconds on high and then stir the ingredients well.
5. Repeat this step until thickened, for a couple of more times.
6. Strain into a clean, large bowl & let chill in the refrigerator for 3 hours, stirring every now and then.
7. In the meantime, over moderate heat settings in a small sauté pan; heat the butter until melted & then add in the pecans & salt, stir well.
8. Toss & cook until toasted, for a couple of minutes; let cool.
9. When completely cooled, pour the mixture into the ice cream maker & process as per the instructions provided by the manufacturer.

10. During the final minutes; add in the pecans.
11. Serve immediately & enjoy.

CHOCOLATE CHUNK AVOCADO ICE CREAM

Prep Time: 10 minutes
Cooking Time: 25 minutes
Servings: 6

Nutritional Value (Estimated Amount Per Serving)

298 Calories
227 Calories from Fat
25g Total Fat
14g Saturated Fat
0.3g Trans Fat
1.3g Polyunsaturated Fat
7.2g Monounsaturated Fat
24mg Cholesterol
32mg Sodium
364mg Potassium
6g Total Carbohydrates
4.7g Dietary Fiber
5.1g Sugars
4.2g Protein

Ingredients

2 Hass avocados, large
½ cup powdered erythritol
6 squares Baker's Chocolate, unsweetened
½ cup cocoa powder, unsweetened
2 tsp. vanilla extract
1 cup coconut milk (from carton)
25 drops of liquid stevia
½ cup heavy whipping cream

Directions

1. Cut the avocados in half and then scoop the avocados out into a large bowl.
2. Add a cup of coconut milk together with 2 tsp. Vanilla Extract & ½ cup of heavy cream; blend this mixture using an immersion blender until completely smooth & creamy, for a minute or two.
3. Grind the erythritol using a spice grinder until completely powdered. Add in the liquid stevia, erythritol & cocoa powder to the avocado mixture; mix well.
4. Once smooth; chop six squares of the unsweetened baker's chocolate & then add them to the bowl. Fold the chocolate in using a large fork or spoon.
5. Place the bowl in a refrigerator and let chill until completely cool, for overnight.
6. Just a couple of minutes before serving; assemble the ice cream machine & follow the manufacturer's instructions.
7. Serve and enjoy.

LOW CARB LEMON CURD ICE CREAM

Prep Time: 10 minutes
Cooking Time: 35 minutes
Servings: 10

Nutritional Value (Estimated Amount Per Serving)

228 Calories
100 Calories from Fat
11g Total Fat
1g Saturated Fat
0.1g Trans Fat
2.4g Polyunsaturated Fat
7.1g Monounsaturated Fat
0mg Cholesterol
252mg Sodium
550mg Potassium
3g Total Carbohydrates
5.4g Dietary Fiber
22g Sugars
3.3g Protein

Ingredients

1 ½ cup heavy whipping cream
2 tbsp vodka
1 recipe lemon curd, chilled
1/3 cup Swerve Sweetener, powdered

Directions

1. Whisk the whipping cream together with lemon curd and powdered Swerve in a large bowl until combined well and then whisk in the vodka as well.
2. Pour the mixture into canister of your ice cream maker & churn as per the directions provided by the manufacturer.
3. Transfer the mixture to an airtight container & freeze for 2 to 3 hours, until firm.

LOW CARB IRISH CREAM ICE CREAM

Prep Time: 15 minutes
Cooking Time: 15 minutes
Servings: 9

Nutritional Value (Estimated Amount Per Serving)

407 Calories
118 Calories from Fat
13g Total Fat
10g Saturated Fat
0g Trans Fat
0.7g Polyunsaturated Fat
1.2g Monounsaturated Fat
62mg Cholesterol
89mg Sodium
188mg Potassium
4g Total Carbohydrates
0.2g Dietary Fiber
36g Sugars
3.7g Protein

Ingredients

2 cups heavy cream
1 tbsp. kahlua syrup, sugar-free
2 tbsp. white chocolate syrup, sugar-free
1 tbsp. chocolate syrup, sugar-free
3 beaten eggs, large
½ tsp. xanthan gum or glucomannan powder
2 cups low-carb Irish cream copycat recipe

Directions

1. Over medium heat settings in a small saucepan; heat the cream for a couple of minutes, until small bubbles starts to form around the edges, stirring frequently.
2. Using a whisk; beat the eggs until light & foamy, for a minute or two. While whisking; slowly drizzle in the hot cream. When have added approximately half of the scalded cream; place cream and eggs to the sauce pan & continue to cook over medium heat settings for a couple of more minutes, until the custard thickens. Strain into a large-sized mixing bowl. Let cool for half an hour. Add in the Low Carb Irish Cream and sweeteners. Whisk in the xanthan or glucomannan. Seal the mixture using a plastic wrap & refrigerate for overnight.
3. Transfer the base into an ice cream mixer. Churn until you get your desired level of thickness. Freeze for a couple of more hours. Serve and enjoy.

KETOGENIC CAKES & MUFFINS

ZUCCHINI CHOCOLATE MUFFINS

Prep Time: 15 minutes
Cooking Time: 35 minutes
Servings: 12

Nutritional Value (Estimated Amount Per Serving)

204 Calories
165 Calories from Fat
18g Total Fat
11g Saturated Fat
0g Trans Fat
1.7g Polyunsaturated Fat
4.4g Monounsaturated Fat
78mg Cholesterol
202mg Sodium
146mg Potassium
5.7g Total Carbohydrates
2.2g Dietary Fiber
2.3g Sugars
5.2g Protein

Ingredients

¾ cup Swerve or any low-carb sweetener
½ tsp. cinnamon
5 organic eggs, large
½ tsp. baking powder
¾ tsp. vanilla extract
½ cup coconut oil or unsalted butter
3 tbsp. cocoa powder, unsweetened
½ cup coconut flour
1 cup zucchini, shredded
½ tsp. baking soda
1 cup almond flour
½ tsp. sea salt

Directions

1. Lightly grease a standard-sized muffin baking mold with 12 cups and preheat your oven to 325 F in advance.
2. Combine sweetener together with coconut oil or butter in a large-sized mixing bowl; mix well.
3. Beat in the eggs and stir in the zucchini, vanilla and cocoa.
4. Mix the remaining ingredients together in a separate bowl.
5. Add dry mix into wet mix; mix well until completely moist.
6. Distribute the prepared batter evenly among the muffin molds.
7. Bake in the preheated oven for 25 to 30 minutes. Immediately remove the muffins from molds & let cool on a wire rack. Serve and enjoy.

BLUEBERRY ZUCCHINI MUFFINS

Prep Time: 10 minutes
Cooking Time: 30 minutes
Servings: 12

Nutritional Value (Estimated Amount Per Serving)

124 Calories
89 Calories from Fat
9.9g Total Fat
2.8g Saturated Fat
0.1g Trans Fat
1.7g Polyunsaturated Fat
4.5g Monounsaturated Fat
37mg Cholesterol
181mg Sodium
171mg Potassium
6.5g Total Carbohydrates
2.4g Dietary Fiber

2.7g Sugars
4.2g Protein

Ingredients

> 1 ½ cups shredded zucchini
> ¼ cup coconut flour
> 1 tsp. baking powder
> ¼ tsp. dried lemon zest
> 1 ½ tsp. cinnamon
> 1 cup blueberries, fresh
> ¼ tsp. baking soda
> 2 eggs, large
> 1 ¼ cup almond flour
> 2 tsp. vanilla extract
> 1 tsp. monk fruit liquid extract
> ½ cup Greek yogurt or sour cream
> 1 ½ tsp. stevia drops
> ½ tsp. sea salt

Directions

1. Stir flours together with cinnamon, baking soda, baking powder, lemon zest and salt in a small bowl. Beat eggs together with monk fruit extract, stevia extract, yogurt or sour cream and vanilla extract in a large bowl for a couple of minutes, until completely smooth.
2. Slowly stir the dry mixture into the wet mix. Fold in the zucchini & then the blueberries. Evenly divide the prepared batter among 12 lined or greased muffin tins.
3. Bake until toothpick comes out clean and browned on top, for 25 to 30 minutes, at 350 F. Let cool for 15 minutes in the pan & then remove the muffins from tins. Let completely cool on the wire rack & enjoy.

LOW CARB BLUEBERRY MUFFINS

Prep Time: 20 minutes
Cooking Time: 40 minute
Servings: 6

Nutritional Value (Estimated Amount Per Serving)

227 Calories
196 Calories from Fat
22g Total Fat
14g Saturated Fat
0.4g Trans Fat
1.1g Polyunsaturated Fat
4.8g Monounsaturated Fat
133mg Cholesterol
307mg Sodium
108mg Potassium
4.4g Total Carbohydrates
1.5g Dietary Fiber
2.2g Sugars
4.6g Protein

Ingredients

> ½ tsp. vanilla
> 4 tbsp. softened cream cheese
> ½ stick softened butter (2 oz)

Wet Ingredients:

> ¼ cup heavy cream
> 3 cold eggs, large

Dry Ingredients:

> ½ cup coconut flour
> 1/16 tsp. cinnamon
> 1 tsp. baking powder
> ¼ cup granulated swerve
> 1/8 tsp. xanthan gum
> ¼ tsp. salt

To Be Added In The Last:

> 2 tsp. granulated swerve
> 1/3 cup blueberries, fresh

Directions

1. Position the oven rack to the lower third of your oven and preheat it to 350 F in advance. Line a 6 cup muffin tin with paper liners. Add the entire dry ingredients together in a small-sized bowl; whisk them together to break up any lumps and well combined.
2. Cream the vanilla together with butter & cream cheese until light and fluffy in a medium-sized bowl. Add an egg into the butter mixture & beat until the mixture turns light & fluffy. Add 1/3 of the dry ingredients; mix until incorporated completely, ensure you get light & fluffy texture.
3. Add one more egg & continue to beat until the batter is fully combined and fluffy. Add half of the leftover dry ingredients and beat again. Add in the leftover egg followed by the remaining dry ingredients; continue to beat until completely incorporated. Finish the process by adding the heavy cream; continue to beat until the batter is thick. Fold in the fresh blueberries.
4. Spoon the prepared batter into a large-sized zip-loc plastic bag & snip off the corner, making approximately ¾" hole. Place the snipped corner into a muffin liner & squeeze the batter into a fat, rounded mound; filling approximately ¾" full; knocking any peaks down with your finger. Sprinkle approximately ¼ tsp. of the Swerve granulated on top of each muffin.
5. Place the tin into the preheated oven. Increase the heat settings to 400 F for a few minutes. Then, set the oven's temperature to 350 F again & bake the blueberry muffins for 25 more minutes. Remove the muffin tin immediately from oven & let cool for 5 minutes.

DELICIOUS NUTS & EGGS MUFFINS

Prep Time: 10 minutes
Cooking Time: 25 minutes
Servings: 12

Nutritional Value (Estimated Amount Per Serving)

162 Calories
124 Calories from Fat
14g Total Fat
2.5g Saturated Fat
0g Trans Fat
3.6g Polyunsaturated Fat
7g Monounsaturated Fat
68mg Cholesterol
87mg Sodium
166mg Potassium
4.8g Total Carbohydrates
1.6g Dietary Fiber
1g Sugars
6.8g Protein

Ingredients

5 eggs, medium, whisked
Spices & stevia to taste
2 cups whole nuts (such as almonds or hazelnuts)
Nutmeg & cinnamon, optional

Directions

1. Grease a standard-sized muffin tray with 12 cups and preheat your oven to 350 F in advance.
2. Process the hazelnuts in a food processor until you get flour like consistency.
3. Whisk the hazelnut flour together with eggs in a large-sized mixing bowl until you get batter like consistency.
4. Add in the spices, stevia and nutmeg & cinnamon, if desired.
5. Fill the muffin tray approximately ¾ full with the prepared batter.
6. Bake in the preheated oven until a cocktail stick comes out clean, for 25 minutes.
7. Let completely cool & enjoy.

DELICIOUS STRAWBERRY MUFFINS

Prep Time: 15 minutes
Cooking Time: 35 minutes
Servings: 12

Nutritional Value (Estimated Amount Per Serving)

226 Calories
180 Calories from Fat
20g Total Fat
5.8g Saturated Fat
0.3g Trans Fat
3.4g Polyunsaturated Fat
9.7g Monounsaturated Fat
67mg Cholesterol
172mg Sodium
212mg Potassium
7.4g Total Carbohydrates
3.2g Dietary Fiber
2.6g Sugars
6.8g Protein

Ingredients

1/3 cup heavy cream
3 large eggs
½ cup swerve sweetener, separated in half
2 ½ cups super fine almond flour (ensure its not a meal)
1 tsp. Cinnamon
2 tsp. fresh baking powder
1 tsp. Vanilla
2/3 cup strawberries, fresh, diced finely
5 tbsp. Butter melted
¼ tsp. pink Himalayan salt

Directions

1. Spray, grease or line a standard-sized muffin tin with papers and preheat your oven to 350 F in advance.
2. Add half of the sugar with strawberries to a large bowl. Mix well & set aside.
3. Beat the sweetener with butter using an electric mixer.
4. Add cream, eggs and vanilla; beat until completely frothy.
5. Sift almond flour together with baking powder, cinnamon & salt. Add the mixture to the wet ingredients; mix until completely combined. Stir in the fresh strawberries.
6. Fill each muffin cup approximately ¾ full with the prepared batter.
7. Bake in the preheated oven until a toothpick comes out clean, for 15 to 20 minutes.

VANILLA STRAWBERRY MUFFIN

Prep Time: 10 minutes
Cooking Time: 25 minutes
Servings: 12

Nutritional Value (Estimated Amount Per Serving)

167 Calories
122 Calories from Fat
14g Total Fat
7.3g Saturated Fat
0.2g Trans Fat
1.1g Polyunsaturated Fat
3.9g Monounsaturated Fat
154mg Cholesterol
145mg Sodium
99mg Potassium
1.6g Total Carbohydrates
0.2g Dietary Fiber
0.8g Sugars
9.6g Protein

Ingredients

2/3 cup strawberries, fresh, chopped
2 cups almond flour
½ cup melted butter
2 tsp. Vanilla essence
¼ cup erythritol
4 organic eggs, large
¼ cup water

2 tsp. baking powder
¼ tsp. salt

Directions

1. Preheat your oven to 350 F in advance.
2. Mix almond flour together with baking powder and salt in a large-sized mixing bowl.
3. Mix butter with water, vanilla essence, erythritol & eggs in a separate bowl.
4. Pour the wet mixture into the dry ingredients; give everything a good stir until evenly mixed. Add in the strawberries.
5. Pour the prepared mixture into the muffin liners.
6. Bake in the preheated oven until firm, for 15 to 20 minutes.
7. Serve & enjoy.

KETO DOUBLE CHOCOLATE AVOCADO MUFFINS

Prep Time: 5 minutes
Cooking Time: 25 minutes
Servings: 10

Nutritional Value (Estimated Amount Per Serving)

228 Calories
157 Calories from Fat
17g Total Fat
5.5g Saturated Fat
0.1g Trans Fat
2.4g Polyunsaturated Fat
8g Monounsaturated Fat
78mg Cholesterol
161mg Sodium
410mg Potassium
9g Total Carbohydrates
5g Dietary Fiber
5.5g Sugars
6.6g Protein

Ingredients

For Wet Ingredients:

2 avocados, medium, peeled, halved & de-seeded
4 large eggs
2 tbsp. heavy cream or coconut milk
15-20 drops of liquid stevia

For Dry Ingredients:

1/3 cup cocoa powder, unsweetened
1 cup almond flour
1/3 cup dark chocolate roughly chopped
1 tsp. cinnamon
1/3 cup coconut flour
1 tsp. baking soda
2 tsp. cream of tartar
½ cup erythritol or any low-carb sweetener

Directions

1. Preheat your oven to 350 F in advance.
2. Place the avocados in a food processor. Pulse on high settings until smooth, for a minute or two.
3. Sift the almond flour together with cacao powder and coconut flour. Add the cream of tartar, erythritol, cinnamon and baking soda; mix well.
4. Add in the coconut milk, eggs, pureed avocado & liquid stevia; process on high settings until combined well.
5. Chop the chocolate roughly & add to the mixture; reserving some pieces for the topic.
6. Scoop the prepared muffin batter into a standard-sized muffin pan lined with paper cups and greased with a small amount of ghee or coconut oil or into a silicone muffin pan.
7. Top the muffins with the kept-aside chocolate pieces & place them in the preheated oven. Bake until the muffins are firm and tops are crispy, for 25 minutes.
8. Immediately remove the pan from oven & let cool on a rack before serving

KETO BANANA NUT MUFFINS

Prep Time: 10 minutes
Cooking Time: 20 minute
Servings: 10

Nutritional Value (Estimated Amount Per Serving)

247 Calories
206 Calories from Fat
23g Total Fat
6.4g Saturated Fat
0.3g Trans Fat
7g Polyunsaturated Fat
8g Monounsaturated Fat
59mg Cholesterol
177mg Sodium
188mg Potassium
6.9g Total Carbohydrates
2.9g Dietary Fiber
1.4g Sugars
6.3g Protein

Ingredients

For Walnut Crumble:

> 1 tbsp. almond flour
> 1 tbsp. cold butter, cut into 4 pieces
> ¾ cup walnuts, chopped
> 1 tbsp. erythritol, powdered

For Muffin Batter:

> 2 large eggs
> 1 ¼ cup almond flour
> 2 tsp. baking powder
> ½ tsp. ground cinnamon
> 2 tbsp. ground flax
> ½ cup powdered erythritol
> 5 tbsp. butter, melted
> ¼ cup almond milk, unsweetened
> 2 ½ tsp. banana extract
> ¼ cup sour cream
> 1 tsp. vanilla extract

Directions

1. Prepare a standard-sized muffin tin, preferably with 10 paper liners; set aside

and then, preheat your oven to 350 F in advance.
2. Combine almond flour together with powdered erythritol, flax, cinnamon and baking powder in a large bowl; mix well.
3. Stir in the vanilla extract, banana extract, butter, sour cream & almond milk.
4. Add eggs to the mixture; give everything a good stir until completely combined.
5. Fill the prepared muffin tins approximately ¾ full with the mixture.

For Crumble Topping:

1. Add almond flour together with walnuts & butter to a food processor.
2. Pulse on high settings until the nuts are chopped into small pieces, a couple of times. Feel free to add one more tbsp. of butter; if the mixture seems to be too dry.
3. Evenly sprinkle bits of the mixture on top of the batter & gently press them down.
4. Sprinkle erythritol over the crumble mixture.
5. Bake in the preheated oven until turn golden & a toothpick comes out clean, for 15 to 20 minutes. Let cool for half an hour, until firm up.
6. Serve and enjoy.

SUGAR-FREE RASPBERRIES MUFFINS

Prep Time: 15 minutes
Cooking Time: 25 minutes
Servings: 8

Nutritional Value (Estimated Amount Per Serving)

116 Calories
80 Calories from Fat
8.9g Total Fat
1.1g Saturated Fat
0g Trans Fat
2.1g Polyunsaturated Fat
5.1g Monounsaturated Fat
70mg Cholesterol

81mg Sodium

153mg Potassium

5.1g Total Carbohydrates

2.8g Dietary Fiber

1.4g Sugars

5.5g Protein

Ingredients

⅛ tsp. baking soda

1 cup blanched almond flour (ensure its not a meal)

3 large eggs

⅛ tsp. vanilla stevia

1 tbsp. lemon zest

¼ cup grape seed oil

1 cup raspberries, frozen

⅛ tsp. Celtic sea salt

Directions

1. Pulse almond flour together with baking soda & salt in a food processor, on high settings.
2. Pulse in lemon zest, eggs, stevia and oil for a few seconds
3. Add the raspberries; give everything a good stir
4. Evenly divide the prepared batter among eight muffins cups
5. Bake for half an hour at 350 F
6. Let cool for half an hour.
7. Serve immediately & enjoy.

CHEESECAKE

Prep Time: 15 minutes

Cooking Time: 1 hour & 30 minutes

Servings: 16 persons

Nutritional Value (Estimated Amount Per Serving)

394 Calories

325 Calories from Fat

36g Total Fat

15g Saturated Fat

0.8g Trans Fat

4.1g Polyunsaturated Fat

13g Monounsaturated Fat

137mg Cholesterol

253mg Sodium

273mg Potassium

8g Total Carbohydrates

2.4g Dietary Fiber

6g Sugars

9.2g Protein

Ingredients

6 ounces almonds, sliced (roughly 1 1/3 cup)

3 tbsp. sweetener, low-carb

5 tbsp. melted salted butter

½ tsp. ground cinnamon optional

For Filling:

3 eggs, large, at room temperature

4 blocks cream cheese softened (roughly 32 ounces)

2 tsp. vanilla extract

¾ cup sweetener, low-carb or to taste

16 ounces sour cream at room temperature

1 tsp. lemon extract optional

Directions

1. Process the sliced almonds in a food processor until finely grounded.
2. Pulse in cinnamon and 6 to 9 packets of stevia extract.
3. Add the melted butter; give everything a good stir.
4. Press into bottom of 9" spring-form pan; set aside

For Filling:

1. Beat the cream cheese until light & fluffy on low speed.
2. Add 24 to 36 stevia extract packets until you get your desired sweetness. Beat on low speed to mix in.
3. Slowly add the eggs, after each addition, don't forget to beat on low.
4. Mix in the extracts and then beat in sour cream on low speed until well incorporated.

5. Spread the prepared cream cheese mixture on top of the crust.

For Cooking:

1. Bake until the top has turned browned, for an hour at 300 F and then turn the oven off.
2. Don't the cheesecake from oven; let it rest there for an hour with door ajar. Remove & transfer on a wire rack to completely cool.
3. Let chill in a refrigerator for a day before serving.

CHOCOLATE CHIP PEANUT BUTTER MUFFINS

Prep Time: 20 minutes
Cooking Time: 25 minutes
Servings: 6

Nutritional Value (Estimated Amount Per Serving)

303 Calories
219 Calories from Fat
24g Total Fat
6.5g Saturated Fat
0g Trans Fat
4.4g Polyunsaturated Fat
11g Monounsaturated Fat
62mg Cholesterol
209mg Sodium
346mg Potassium
13g Total Carbohydrates
5.2g Dietary Fiber
2.4g Sugars
11g Protein

Ingredients

1/3 cup peanut butter
1 tsp. baking powder
½ cup erythritol
1 cup almond flour
½ cup sugar-free chocolate chips or cacao nibs
2 organic eggs, large
1/3 cup almond milk
A pinch of Himalayan pink salt

Directions

1. Preheat your oven to 350 F in advance.
2. Combine the entire dry ingredients together (don't add the cacao nibs) in a large-sized mixing bowl; give everything a good stir until completely combined.
3. Add almond milk and peanut butter; stir well.
4. Slowly add in the eggs and stir until completely combined (stirring after every addition).
5. Fold in the sugar-free chocolate chips or cacao nibs.
6. Spray a standard-sized muffin tin with the cooking oil spray & distribute the batter evenly.
7. Bake in the preheated oven for 25 to 30 minutes; set aside and let completely cool. Serve and enjoy.

CHOCOLATE CHEESECAKE

Prep Time: 30 minutes
Cooking Time: 55 minutes
Servings: 8

Nutritional Value (Estimated Amount Per Serving)

498 Calories
387 Calories from Fat
43g Total Fat
21g Saturated Fat
0.3g Trans Fat
3.5g Polyunsaturated Fat
14g Monounsaturated Fat
139mg Cholesterol
368mg Sodium
270mg Potassium
10g Total Carbohydrates
2.5g Dietary Fiber
12g Sugars
10g Protein

Ingredients

For Chocolate Crust

1 tbsp. cocoa powder

4 tbsp. butter
1/16 tsp. Stevia
1 cup almond flour
½ tsp. cinnamon
A pinch of salt

For Cheesecake Filling

16 oz cream cheese softened
¾ cup erythritol
2 eggs, large
½ cup sour cream
3 oz baker's chocolate, unsweetened
1 tbsp. cocoa powder
A pinch of salt
1 tsp. vanilla extract

Directions

1. Preheat your oven to 350 F in advance.
2. For Crust: Heat 4 tbsp. of butter until melted completely and then combine with the cocoa powder, almond flour, Stevia and cinnamon; mix well. Press the crust dough into a 9" spring form pan & bake in the preheated oven until the crust is dark and solid, for 15 minutes.
3. In the meantime, start making the cheesecake filling. Using an electric hand mixer; beat the cream cheese with erythritol until smooth.
4. Add vanilla extract, sour cream, 2 eggs and salt; beat for a minute or two, until creamy.
5. Over low heat settings in a small pan or in a double boiler; melt 3 oz. of unsweetened baker's chocolate, stirring continuously.
6. Pour 1 tbsp. of cocoa powder and the chocolate into your cream cheese mixture. Give everything a good stir using a rubber spatula/spoon until the cream cheese mixture & chocolate combines together.
7. Pour the cheesecake batter into the spring-form pan on top of crisp almond flour crust
8. Bake until the top of the cheesecake is dark and set, but still jiggly underneath, for 50 to 55 minutes
9. Let the cheesecake to cool at room temperature and then refrigerate for overnight.

10. When done, loosen any cake that has stuck to the pan by running a plastic knife along the edges of the spring-form pan. Undo the buckle and remove the pan's edges.
11. Slice and serve with a square of dark chocolate and some whipped cream. Enjoy!

FUDGY BROWNIES

Prep Time: 20 minutes
Cooking Time: 30 minutes
Servings: 20 persons

Nutritional Value (Estimated Amount Per Serving)

362 Calories
191 Calories from Fat
43g Total Fat
24g Saturated Fat
0.1g grams Trans Fat
3.7g Polyunsaturated Fat
13g Monounsaturated Fat
175mg Cholesterol
151mg Sodium
373mg Potassium
9g Total Carbohydrates
4g Dietary Fiber
12g Sugars
9.3g Protein

Ingredients

For Classic Fudgy Keto Brownies

6 oz. dark chocolate at least 80%
3 tbsp. walnuts or any other nuts, coarsely ground
6 tbsp. butter unsalted
¾ cup sweetener powdered
2 oz. almond flour
4 large eggs, at room temperature
½ tsp. baking powder
2 tbsp. chocolate chunks optional
½ tsp. vanilla extract
2 tbsp. coconut oil
A dash of salt or to taste

For Keto Brownies

> *8 oz. dark chocolate at least 80%*
> *6 tbsp. butter unsalted*
> *2 large egg yolks room temperature*
> *3 large eggs room temperature*
> *2 tbsp. coconut oil*
> *¾ cup sweetener powdered*
> *2 tbsp. chocolate chunks*
> *½ tsp. vanilla extract*
> *3 tbsp. walnuts or any other nuts, coarsely ground*
> *A dash of salt*

Directions

1. Line a standard-sized baking pan, preferably 8 x8" with parchment paper and preheat your oven to 330 F in advance.
2. Put coconut oil together with chocolate & butter in a microwave-safe bowl. Microwave for 1 ½ minute until completely melted. Remove and then give the mixture a good stir until uniform. Set aside until easy to handle. Combine eggs together with vanilla extract, erythritol & salt using an electric mixer. Mix for 2 to 3 minutes, on high.
3. Carefully whisk in the chocolate mixture until just combined.
4. Now, sift and stir the baking powder & almond flour in a small bowl.
5. Now mix the flour into the chocolate-egg mixture until combined well.
6. Pour the prepared mixture into the baking pan & evenly spread it out using a large spatula.
7. Sprinkle with some chopped chocolate and/or crushed walnuts, if desired.
8. Bake in the preheated oven until a toothpick comes out clean, for 15 to 20 minutes; ensure that you don't over-bake else it would burn.
9. When done; remove & set aside at room temperature to cool down completely then, cut into 20 brownies, preferably equal size. Serve & enjoy.

PEANUT BUTTER FUDGE

Prep Time: 10 minutes
Cooking Time: 10 minutes
Servings: 12 persons

Nutritional Value (Estimated Amount Per Serving)

296 Calories
264 Calories from Fat
29g Total Fat
17g Saturated Fat
0g Trans Fat
2.5g Polyunsaturated Fat
7.1g Monounsaturated Fat
0mg Cholesterol
79mg Sodium
145mg Potassium
4.8g Total Carbohydrates
1.9g Dietary Fiber
1.1g Sugars
5.6g Protein

Ingredients

> *1 cup peanut butter, unsweetened*
> *¼ cup vanilla almond milk, unsweetened*
> *1 cup coconut oil*

Optional Ingredients:

> *2 tsp. liquid vanilla stevia*
> *A pinch of salt*

Chocolate Sauce Topping (optional):

> *2 tbsp. coconut oil, melted*
> *¼ cup cocoa powder, unsweetened*
> *2 tbsp. Swerve*

Directions

1. Slightly soften or melt the coconut oil and peanut butter on the stove or in the microwave, on low heat settings.
2. Add the mixture with the remaining ingredients to your blender; blend on high settings until well combined.

3. Pour into a loaf pan lined with a parchment.
4. Refrigerate for a couple of hours, until set.
5. Whisk the chocolate sauce ingredients together and then drizzle the mixture over the fudge (once the fudge is completely set). Refrigerate until ready to serve.

CHOCOLATE TRUFFLE TORTE

Prep Time: 5 minutes
Cooking Time: 35 minutes
Servings: 8 persons

Nutritional Value (Estimated Amount Per Serving)

432 Calories
384 Calories from Fat
54g Total Fat
32g Saturated Fat
0.6g Trans Fat
2.6g Polyunsaturated Fat
16g Monounsaturated Fat
249mg Cholesterol
110mg Sodium
325mg Potassium
10g Total Carbohydrates
3.1g Dietary Fiber
23g Sugars
8.3g Protein

Ingredients

2/3 cup heavy cream
A bar of 85% Dark Chocolate
3 organic eggs, large
1 tbsp. cocoa, sifted
½ cup granular Splenda
1 tsp. vanilla
½ cup cut up butter, unsalted
A pinch of salt

Directions

1. Over low heat settings in a pot; melt the chocolate bar and butter (don't let it bubble), stirring every now and then.

Whisk for a minute or two, until smooth completely. Whisk sweetener (splenda) together with cocoa, eggs, vanilla, cream and salt in a separate bowl. Add butter-chocolate mixture to wet ingredients; blend until well incorporated and then pour the mixture into a lightly greased 9″ pie plate.

2. Bake until the center of the cake is almost firm to the touch and still jiggly slightly but the torte has puffed around the edges, for 15 minutes at 350 F. Let cool at room temperature for a couple of minutes and then transfer in a refrigerator to chill. Serve with raspberries and sugar free whipped cream.

ULTIMATE COFFEE CAKE

Prep Time: 35 minutes
Cooking Time: 25 minutes
Servings: 6

Nutritional Value (Estimated Amount Per Serving)

348 Calories
245 Calories from Fat
27g Total Fat
9.9g Saturated Fat
0.3g Trans Fat
3.8g Polyunsaturated Fat
11g Monounsaturated Fat
177mg Cholesterol
180mg Sodium
294mg Potassium
15g Total Carbohydrates
3.2g Dietary Fiber
8.2g Sugars
13g Protein

Ingredients

For Base:

¼ cup protein powder, unflavored
6 eggs, separated
¼ tsp. liquid stevia
6 oz. cream cheese

¼ tsp. cream of tartar

2 tsp. vanilla extract

¼ cup erythritol

For Filling:

½ stick butter

1 ½ cup almond flour

¼ cup erythritol

1 tbsp. cinnamon

¼ cup maple syrup substitute

Directions

1. Preheat your oven to 325 F in advance. Separate the eggs from egg whites and then cream the egg yolks with erythritol; add the remaining ingredients (except for egg whites and cream of tartar) whisk well.
2. Whip the cream of tartar and egg whites until stiff peaks form.
3. Fold ½ of the egg white mixture into the yolks and then the other half.
4. Mix the entire filling ingredients together until a dough forms.
5. Pour the base batter into dark metal cake pan and top with half of the cinnamon filling; pushing it down.
6. Bake in the preheated oven for 20 minutes and then top the cake with the remaining filling dough.
7. Bake until a toothpick comes out clean, for 20 to 30 more minutes. Before removing the cake from pan; let it cool for a couple of minutes.

PUMPKIN LOAF CAKE

Prep Time: 10 minutes
Cooking Time: 90 minutes
Servings: 10

Nutritional Value (Estimated Amount Per Serving)

146 Calories

100 Calories from Fat

11g Total Fat

2.9g Saturated Fat

0g Trans Fat

2.2g Polyunsaturated Fat

5.5g Monounsaturated Fat

0mg Cholesterol

233mg Sodium

267mg Potassium

10g Total Carbohydrates

5.2g Dietary Fiber

1.7g Sugars

6g Protein

Ingredients

¼ cup Psyllium husk powder

1 ½ cup almond flour

½ cup coconut milk (from the carton)

3 egg whites, large

¼ cup Swerve sweetener

2 tsp. baking powder

½ cup pumpkin puree

1 ½ tsp. pumpkin pie spice

½ tsp. kosher salt

Directions

1. Sift the entire dry ingredients together in a large bowl. Place a container with approximately 1 cup water on the bottom rack and then preheat your oven to 350 F in advance.
2. Add coconut milk and pumpkin into dry ingredients; mix well until evenly coated. Whip the egg whites up for a minute or two, until stiff and then slowly fold egg whites into the dough.
3. Spread the dough into a loaf pan, well-greased and then bake in the preheated oven for 75 minutes.
4. Let them cool a bit at room temperature and then slice. Serve warm and enjoy.

BLUEBERRY MUFFINS

Prep Time: 25 minutes
Cooking Time: 55 minutes
Servings: 12

Nutritional Value (Estimated Amount Per Serving)

450 Calories
380 Calories from Fat
42g Total Fat
16g Saturated Fat
0.8g Trans Fat
5.9g Polyunsaturated Fat
18g Monounsaturated Fat
127mg Cholesterol
177mg Sodium
347mg Potassium
13g Total Carbohydrates
5g Dietary Fiber
4.1g Sugars
11g Protein

Ingredients

2 cups almond flour
¼ cup melted butter
1 cup heavy whipping cream, organic (without added carbs)
½ tsp. pure lemon extract
2 organic eggs, large
½ cup blueberries, fresh
5 drops of liquid Stevia or to taste
1 tsp. baking powder
¼ tsp. lemon zest

Directions

1. Preheat your oven to 350 F in advance
2. Melt the butter and zest the lemon
3. Crack eggs in a large-sized mixing bowl; whisk until mixed well
4. Add the entire ingredients together into the mixing bowl & mix until combined well
5. Fill the muffins tin (with 12 silicone baking cups) approximately ¾ full with the batter.
6. Bake in the preheated oven until a toothpick comes out clean and turn golden brown, for 25 to 30 minutes.

PANCAKES

Prep Time: 20 minutes
Cooking Time: 20 minutes
Servings: 1

Nutritional Value (Estimated Amount Per Serving)

384 Calories
296 Calories from Fat
33g Total Fat
18g Saturated Fat
0g Trans Fat
2.8g Polyunsaturated Fat
8.9g Monounsaturated Fat
429mg Cholesterol
322mg Sodium
251mg Potassium
7.3g Total Carbohydrates
1.7g Dietary Fiber
3g Sugars
17g Protein

Ingredients

2 eggs, large
½ to 1 packet Stevia
2 oz cream cheese, organic
1 tbsp. coconut flour
½ tsp. cinnamon

Directions

1. Beat or blend the entire ingredients until smooth.
2. Over medium-high heat settings in a non-stick skillet or pan; heat the coconut oil or butter.
3. Once hot; drop the batter into the hot oil and cook for a couple of minutes; flip and cook the other side as well until cooked through.

4. Top the pancake with a sugar-free maple syrup and/or butter.

LAVA CAKE

Prep Time: 15 minutes
Cooking Time: 15 minutes
Servings: 1 person

Nutritional Value (Estimated Amount Per Serving)

172 Calories
95 Calories from Fat
11g Total Fat
4.8g Saturated Fat
0.2g Trans Fat
1.1g Polyunsaturated Fat
3g Monounsaturated Fat
181mg Cholesterol
338mg Sodium
79mg Potassium
9.8g Total Carbohydrates
2g Dietary Fiber
1g Sugars
8g Protein

Ingredients

2 tbsp. cocoa powder
½ tsp. vanilla extract
1 organic egg, medium
1-2 tbsp. erythritol
¼ tsp. baking powder
1 tbsp. heavy cream
A pinch of salt

Directions

1. Preheat your oven to 350 F in advance. Combine cocoa powder with erythritol; whisk well until smooth and make sure there are no clumps.
2. Beat the egg in a separate bowl until fluffy. Add egg, vanilla extract and heavy cream to the cocoa-erythritol mixture. Add baking powder and salt as well.

3. Lightly coat the mug with the cooking oil, pour the batter and bake at 350 F until set but pretty jiggly, for 10 to 15 minutes. Don't overcook the cake.
4. Top the cake with whipped cream, ice cream, or any type of goodies. For molten lava cake; add a scoop of ice cream to the top of the mug, while still hot.

BANANA WALNUT BREAD

Prep Time: 10 minutes
Cooking Time: 1 hour & 5 minutes
Servings: 10 persons

Nutritional Value (Estimated Amount Per Serving)

553 Calories
412 Calories from Fat
46g Total Fat
7.1g Saturated Fat
0g Trans Fat
12g Polyunsaturated Fat
24g Monounsaturated Fat
112mg Cholesterol
296mg Sodium
669mg Potassium
11g Total Carbohydrates
8.1g Dietary Fiber
7g Sugars
12g Protein

Ingredients

2 cups almond flour
1 tsp. baking soda
3 bananas, medium
½ cup walnuts
3 eggs, large
¼ cup olive oil
Coconut oil

Directions

1. Lightly grease a loaf pan with the coconut oil and preheat your oven to 350 F in advance.

2. Cut up the bananas and then add the entire ingredients in a large-sized mixing bowl; mix until combined well.
3. Pour the mixture into the prepared loaf pan and bake for 55 to 60 minutes.

LEMON CUPCAKES WITH BERRY FROSTING

Prep Time: 10 minutes
Cooking Time: 55 minutes
Servings: 12 persons

Nutritional Value (Estimated Amount Per Serving)

335 Calories
274 Calories from Fat
30g Total Fat
12g Saturated Fat
0.2g Trans Fat
3.8g Polyunsaturated Fat
12g Monounsaturated Fat
99mg Cholesterol
306mg Sodium
251mg Potassium
8.7g Total Carbohydrates
3.4g Dietary Fiber
3.3g Sugars
8.8g Protein

Ingredients

For Lemon Cupcakes:

2 tsp. lemon extract
1 tsp. baking powder
3 eggs, large
½ tsp. xanthan gum
2 1/3 cups almond flour
¾ cup almond milk, unsweetened
2 tbsp. butter, melted
¾ cup erythritol blend/granulated stevia
2 tbsp. lemon zest
1 tbsp. vanilla extract
½ tsp. sea salt

For Raspberry Frosting:

3 tbsp. whipping cream
1/3 cup erythritol blend/granulated stevia
1 tsp. lemon juice, fresh
16 ounces cream cheese, softened
¾ cup raspberries, frozen, unsweetened
2 tbsp. butter, softened
1 tsp. vanilla extract

Directions

1. Line a standard-sized cupcake pan with papers and preheat your oven at 350 F in advance.
2. Whisk almond flour together with xanthan gum, baking powder, zest, salt and sweetener in a large bowl, until combined well.
3. Whisk melted butter into the dry ingredients; whisk well until coarse crumbs form.
4. Add eggs; give everything a good stir until the batter begins to stick together and well incorporated.
5. Add almond milk, lemon extract & vanilla; whisk until the batter is smooth.
6. Fill the prepared cupcake papers approximately ¾ full with the batter.
7. Place the cupcakes into the preheated oven & bake until the cupcake bounces back when pressed, for 30 to 32 minutes.
8. Let the cupcakes to cool on a rack before starting the frosting process.
9. Using an electric mixer; whip the cream cheese together with butter in a large bowl.
10. Blend in frozen raspberries and sweetener until well combined.
11. Add in the lemon juice, whipping cream & vanilla; blend until completely smooth.
12. Frost the cupcakes using a piping bag.

BREAD PUDDING

Prep Time: 15 minutes
Cooking Time: 45 minutes
Servings: 1 batch

Nutritional Value (Estimated Amount Per Serving)

145 Calories
76 Calories from Fat
8.4g Total Fat
4.6g Saturated Fat
0.1g Trans Fat
0.8g Polyunsaturated Fat
2.6g Monounsaturated Fat
62mg Cholesterol
95mg Sodium
51mg Potassium
8g Total Carbohydrates
0.9g Dietary Fiber
8.8g Sugars
3g Protein

Ingredients

3 organic eggs, large
1½ cups almond milk, unsweetened
30 g mini chocolate chips, low-carb
6 slices cinnamon bread; cut into cubes
¼ cup sweetener, low-carb
4 tbsp unsalted butter

Directions

1. Preheat your oven to 375 F in advance.
2. Place the cubed bread into a large-sized bowl.
3. Over moderate heat settings in a large saucepan; heat up the milk until it starts boil; decrease the heat settings & then add in the butter. Give everything a good stir until the butter is completely melted.
4. Pour the milk mixture over the bread; set aside & let soak for 10 to 12 minutes.
5. Combine eggs together with sweetener in a separate bowl.
6. Pour the prepared egg mixture over the bread & then add in the chocolate chips.
7. Pour everything together into a large-sized baking dish, preferably greased lightly with the butter; pushing down the bread and ensure that it's completely in the liquid.
8. Bake in the preheated oven until the egg mixture has set, for half an hour. Let cool for a couple of minutes and then serve.

CHOCOLATE MUFFINS

Prep Time: 15 minutes
Cooking Time: 25 minutes
Servings: 12 persons

Nutritional Value (Estimated Amount Per Serving)

115 Calories
75 Calories from Fat
8.3g Total Fat
4.5g Saturated Fat
0.2g Trans Fat
0.6g Polyunsaturated Fat
2.2g Monounsaturated Fat
78mg Cholesterol
128mg Sodium
71mg Potassium
5.5g Total Carbohydrates
1.3g Dietary Fiber
1.7g Sugars
4.6g Protein

Ingredients

4 eggs, large
1 ounce Lily's chocolate
¼ cup cocoa powder
1 ounce 100% bakers cocoa bar
¼ cup erythritol
4 tbsp. butter
½ cup peanut flour
1 tsp. baking powder
¼ cup heavy cream
1 tsp. vanilla
1/8 tsp salt

Directions

1. Combine the entire dry ingredients together in a large-sized mixing bowl. Thoroughly mix the peanut flour with erythritol, cocoa powder, baking powder & salt.
2. Combine butter with heavy cream using a hand mixer in a separate medium-sized bowl.
3. Once completely combined; add vanilla and eggs; mix until well combined.
4. Add the dry ingredients to the wet; mix until well combined.
5. Add ½ of the Lilly's chocolate and the bakers chocolate completely and fold together.
6. Scoop the batter into the muffin tins & top each cup with the leftover Lilly's chocolate.
7. Bake until a toothpick comes out clean, for 20 minutes at 350. Serve and enjoy.

GLUTEN-FREE CHOCOLATE COCONUT CUPCAKES

Prep Time: 15 minutes
Cooking Time: 25 minutes
Servings: 20 persons

Nutritional Value (Estimated Amount Per Serving)

393 Calories
365 Calories from Fat
41g Total Fat
23g Saturated Fat
0g Trans Fat
2.1g Polyunsaturated Fat
13g Monounsaturated Fat
115mg Cholesterol
81mg Sodium
65mg Potassium
6.1g Total Carbohydrates
1.6g Dietary Fiber
3.4g Sugars
2.9g Protein

Ingredients

For Cupcakes:

1 cup coconut flour, sifted
½ tsp. paleo baking powder
A pinch of Himalayan Pink sea salt
½ tsp. baking soda
8 small-medium sized eggs or 7 large eggs
½ cup cacao butter
2 tsp. vanilla powder
1 cup xylitol
½ cup cocoa powder
1 tsp. apple cider vinegar
2 tsp. cinnamon
1 pound grass-fed butter or ghee

For Icing:

1/3 cup coconut cream
Xylitol
¼ cocoa powder
2-3 tbsp. Brain Octane Oil
¼ cup cacao butter
A pinch of salt

For Garnish:

Fresh berries

Directions

1. Line 2 standard-sized trays of muffin tins with paper cups and then, preheat your oven to 350 F in advance.
2. Over moderate heat settings in a small saucepan; combine the butter with cacao powder until the butter is completely melted & well incorporated.
3. Add the entire ingredients to a food processor; blend on high settings until completely smooth & creamy.
4. Taste & adjust the amount of sweetness, if required; adding a pinch more of salt to enhance the chocolate flavor or a touch of more sweetener, cinnamon or vanilla.
5. Fill pre-prepared muffin trays evenly with the mixture.
6. Place in the preheated oven & bake roughly for 15 to 20 minutes.

7. In the meantime, add the entire icing ingredients together to a small-sized saucepan & heat it over low to medium heat settings until combined completely.
8. Taste & adjust the amount of sweetness, if required. Pour the mixture into a large bowl and then place in a fridge until completely set.
9. When the muffins are cooked through & turn golden brown, immediately remove them from the oven; set aside and let cool.
10. Remove the chilled icing from fridge & spread on top of the cooled muffins; garnish the cup-cakes with fresh berries. Serve and enjoy.

LOW-CARB MATCHA COCONUT CUPCAKES

Prep Time: 15 minutes
Cooking Time: 25 minutes
Servings: 6 persons

Nutritional Value (Estimated Amount Per Serving)

221 Calories
159 Calories from Fat
18g Total Fat
8.1g Saturated Fat
0g Trans Fat
2.2g Polyunsaturated Fat
6.6g Monounsaturated Fat
0mg Cholesterol
274mg Sodium
213mg Potassium
14g Total Carbohydrates
1.8g Dietary Fiber
4.8g Sugars
4.4g Protein

Ingredients

For The Cupcakes:
¼ cup plus 1 tbsp. coconut flour
1 tsp. vanilla extract
½ cup coconut butter/manna

1 tsp. baking powder
¼ cup Swerve, or other granulated sweetener
1 tbsp. ground flax seeds
½ cup hot water
A pinch of salt

For The Frosting:

½ tsp. matcha powder
1 cup cashews, raw
2 tbsp Swerve
1 tsp. vanilla extract
½ cup coconut milk, full-fat

Directions

For The Cupcakes:

1. Line or grease a small-sized muffin tin (with 6 wells) and then preheat your oven to 350 F in advance.
2. Pour water over the coconut butter & stir until completely smooth & well combined.
3. Mix in the vanilla, flax, salt and Swerve. Set aside and let sit for a couple of minutes
4. Combine coconut flour with baking powder in a separate bowl.
5. Slowly add in the flour mixture; stir until evenly combined & no lumps remain.
6. Evenly divide the mixture into the muffin tins & bake in the preheated oven until the edges are just beginning to turn golden and the tops are firm, for 20 to 25 minutes.
7. Remove & set aside for a couple of hours and prepare the frosting.

For The Frosting:

1. Dump the entire ingredients together in a high-power blender & blend on high settings for a minute or two, until completely smooth. Spoon the mixture on top of the chilled cupcakes. Sprinkle with dried coconut. Serve immediately and enjoy.

KETO SWEET FAT-BOMBS

BLUEBERRY FAT BOMBS

Prep Time: 5 minutes
Cooking Time: 1 hour & 35 minutes
Servings: 14

Nutritional Information (Estimated Amount Per Serving)

216 Calories
196 Calories from Fat
22g Total Fat
16g Saturated Fat
0.3g Trans Fat
0.6g Polyunsaturated Fat
3.2g Monounsaturated Fat
26mg Cholesterol
80mg Sodium
26mg Potassium
4.9g Total Carbohydrates
0.3g Dietary Fiber
4.1g Sugars
0.7g Protein

Ingredients

¼ cup coconut cream
4 oz butter (1 stick), softened
1 scant cup of fresh blueberries (approximately 9/10 cup)
4 oz. cream cheese, softened
¾ cup coconut oil
Preferred Sweetener to taste

Directions

1. Place berries together with softened cream cheese and coconut cream in a blender or food processor; puree on high settings until completely smooth. Melt the coconut oil and butter over low heat settings in a large saucepan. Set aside for 5 minutes to cool slightly and add the mixture to the blender or food processor. Puree on high settings again until completely smooth.

2. Slowly add your favorite sweetener. Taste & adjust the amount of sweetener to your preference. Transfer the prepared mixture to a spouted measuring cup & gently fill the molds approximately 1/3 with the prepared mixture. Freeze for an hour, until set (keep them refrigerated until ready to serve). When ready to serve; simply pop them out & enjoy.

WHITE CHOCOLATE COCONUT FUDGE

Prep Time: 15 minutes
Cooking Time: 10 minutes
Servings: 24

Nutritional Information (Estimated Amount Per Serving)

199 Calories
182 Calories from Fat
20g Total Fat
16g Saturated Fat
0g Trans Fat
0.3g Polyunsaturated Fat
2.3g Monounsaturated Fat
0.3mg Cholesterol
15mg Sodium
109mg Potassium
3.3g Total Carbohydrates
1.9g Dietary Fiber
0.9g Sugars
2.7g Protein

Ingredients

1 cup coconut butter
4 ounces cacao butter
1 can coconut milk (15 ounce)
½ cup coconut oil
1 tsp. vanilla extract
A pinch of salt

1 tsp. coconut liquid stevia
½ cup vanilla protein powder

For Topping:

Unsweetened coconut flakes

Directions

1. Over low heat settings in a large sauce pan; heat the cacao butter until completely melted.
2. Stir in the coconut oil, coconut milk & coconut butter.
3. Give everything a good stir until no lumps remain & the mixture is completely smooth.
4. Turn off the heat settings & whisk is the stevia, vanilla extract, protein powder & salt.
5. Pour the prepared mixture into 8x8" pan lined with parchment paper.
6. Sprinkle coconut flakes over the top.
7. Refrigerate for overnight or for 4 hours.

ALMOND PISTACHIO FAT BOMBS

Prep Time: 20 minutes
Cooking Time: 50 minutes
Servings: 36

Nutritional Information (Estimated Amount Per Serving)

155 Calories
147 Calories from Fat
16g Total Fat
12g Saturated Fat
0g Trans Fat
0.5g Polyunsaturated Fat
2.4g Monounsaturated Fat
3.6mg Cholesterol
18mg Sodium
58mg Potassium
2.1g Total Carbohydrates
1.3g Dietary Fiber
0.7g Sugars
0.8g Protein

Ingredients

¼ tsp. pure almond extract
1 cup roasted almond butter, all natural
½ cup cacao butter, chopped finely & melted
1 cup creamy coconut butter
½ cup coconut milk, full fat, chilled for overnight
1 cup coconut oil, firm
¼ cup ghee
1 tbsp. pure vanilla extract
¼ cup raw pistachios, shelled, chopped
2 tsp. chai spice
¼ tsp. Himalayan pink salt

Directions

1. Grease & line a 9 inch square baking pan with the parchment paper. For easy unmolding; don't forget to leave a little bit hanging on either side; set aside.
2. Now, over low heat settings in a small saucepan; heat the cacao butter until completely melted, stirring often; reserve.
3. Add the entire leftover ingredients (don't add the shelled pistachios and cacao butter) to a mixing bowl, preferably large-sized. Mix well using a hand mixer until the mixture becomes light and airy and the entire ingredients are combined well (beginning with the lowest possible speed & slowly increasing the speed to high).
4. Transfer the melted cacao butter into the almond mixture; continue to mix until well incorporated, on low speed.
5. Transfer to the prepared mixture to pan, evenly spread & sprinkle chopped pistachios over the top.
6. Refrigerate for overnight, until completely set. Once done; cut into 36 equal sized squares. Serve and enjoy.

EASY LEMON FAT BOMBS

Prep Time: 5 minutes
Cooking Time: 55 minutes
Servings: 16

Nutritional Information (Estimated Amount Per Serving)

115 Calories
105 Calories from Fat
12g Total Fat
10g Saturated Fat
0g Trans Fat
0.1g Polyunsaturated Fat
0.6g Monounsaturated Fat
0mg Cholesterol
13mg Sodium
71mg Potassium
7.5g Total Carbohydrates
2.1g Dietary Fiber
1g Sugars
0.9g Protein

Ingredients

15 to 20 drops of Stevia extract (Lemon or Clear)
2 oz extra virgin coconut oil, softened (¼ cup), at room temperature
7.1 oz coconut butter, softened, at room temperature
1-2 tbsp. lemon extract or lemon zest, organic
A pinch of Himalayan pink salt or sea salt

Directions

1. Mix the entire ingredients together in a large bowl & ensure the stevia and lemon zest are evenly distributed.
2. Fill each silicone candy mold or mini muffin paper cup with approximately 1 tbsp. of the prepared coconut mixture & place on a tray.
3. Place the tray inside the fridge and let chill until firm, for 40 to 50 minutes.
4. Keep refrigerated until ready to serve. Serve and enjoy.

SPICED COCOA COOLERS AKA FROZEN FAT BOMBS

Prep Time: 20 minutes
Cooking Time: 2 hours & 20 minutes
Servings: 10

Nutritional Information (Estimated Amount Per Serving)

95 Calories
79 Calories from Fat
8.7g Total Fat
5.5g Saturated Fat
0.3g Trans Fat
0.4g Polyunsaturated Fat
2.2g Monounsaturated Fat
27mg Cholesterol
18mg Sodium
26mg Potassium
10g Total Carbohydrates
0.4g Dietary Fiber
0.8g Sugars
1g Protein

Ingredients

8 fl oz coconut milk or heavy whipping cream (1 cup)
1 tsp. cinnamon
0.4 oz unsweetened cocoa powder (2 tbsp.)
1 tsp. unsweetened vanilla extract or 1 vanilla bean
0.7 oz Swerve or Erythritol (2 tbsp.)
¼ tsp. cayenne pepper
15-20 drops of Stevia extract (Chocolate /Vanilla /Clear)

Directions

1. Slightly heat up the coconut milk or cream over moderate heat settings in a large saucepan until Luke warm.
2. Place the entire ingredients into the coconut milk or cream; mix until combined well.
3. Pour the prepared liquid into an ice-cube tray (filling with approximately 1 tbsp. per piece) & place the tray into the freezer. Let

sit until completely frozen, for a couple of hours
4. Serve immediately & enjoy.

MACADAMIA CHOCOLATE FAT BOMB

Prep Time: 10 minutes
Cooking Time: 1 hour & 30 minutes
Servings: 6

Nutritional Information (Estimated Amount Per Serving)

307 Calories
296 Calories from Fat
33g Total Fat
15g Saturated Fat
0g Trans Fat
0.7g Polyunsaturated Fat
15g Monounsaturated Fat
0mg Cholesterol
0.9mg Sodium
70mg Potassium
3.6g Total Carbohydrates
2g Dietary Fiber
0.9g Sugars
1.8g Protein

Ingredients

2 oz cocoa butter
4 oz macadamias, chopped
2 tbsp. Swerve
¼ cup coconut oil or heavy cream
2 tbsp. cocoa powder, unsweetened

Directions

1. Fill a large sauce pan half full with the boiling water. Place a small sized saucepan over the large sauce pan with the boiling water and melt the cocoa butter in it.
2. Once melted; add in the cocoa powder and then add the Swerve; mix well until the entire ingredients are completely melted and well blended.

3. Add in the macadamias; give everything a good stir.
4. Now, add the cream or coconut oil; mix well (bringing back to the temperature). Pour the mixture in paper candy cups or molds. Let cool for a couple of minutes at room temperature and then place in a refrigerator. Let chill until harden. Serve and enjoy.

KETO COCONUT FAT BOMBS

Prep Time: 10 minutes
Cooking Time: 50 minutes
Servings: 12

Nutritional Information (Estimated Amount Per Serving)

119 Calories
100 Calories from Fat
11g Total Fat
8.8g Saturated Fat
0.2g Trans Fat
0.3g Polyunsaturated Fat
1.4g Monounsaturated Fat
10mg Cholesterol
65mg Sodium
35mg Potassium
12g Total Carbohydrates
0.9g Dietary Fiber
3.5g Sugars
0.3g Protein

Ingredients

2 oz extra virgin coconut oil (¼ cup, at room temperature)
4 oz unsweetened flaked coconut or desiccated, shredded coconut (1 ½ cup)
¼ tsp. vanilla bean powder or cinnamon
2 oz butter, grass-fed; softened & chopped into pieces (¼ cup, at room temperature)
20-25 drops of Stevia extract
A pinch of celtic salt

Directions

1. Preheat your oven to 350 F in advance. Spread the flaked or shredded coconut on a large-sized baking sheet. Toast in the preheated oven until turn light golden, for 5 to 8 minutes (To prevent them from burning; don't forget to mix them once or twice during the toasting process).
2. Add them to the bowl of a blender & pulse on high settings until smooth.
3. Add in the coconut oil & butter then add vanilla or cinnamon, salt and stevia; mix well.
4. Pour the prepared mixture into an ice cube tray or mini muffin forms (filling each one with approximately 1 ½ tbsp. of the mixture). Place in the fridge & let sit until solidify, for half an hour or more. Keep refrigerated until ready to serve.

COCONUT ALMOND FAT BOMBS

Prep Time: 5 minutes
Cooking Time: 45 minutes
Servings: 15

Nutritional Info (Estimated Amount Per Serving)

108 Calories
72 Calories from Fat
7.5g Total Fat
5.6g Saturated Fat
0g Trans Fat
0.2g Polyunsaturated Fat
1.6g Monounsaturated Fat
15mg Cholesterol
49mg Sodium
76mg Potassium
6.3g Total Carbohydrates
1.2g Dietary Fiber
2.9g Sugars
3.6g Protein

Ingredients

1.7 ounces butter, unsalted
¾ tsp. cardamom
14 ounces ricotta
½ tsp. vanilla extract, unsweetened
1 tbsp. psyllium husk
1/3 cup coconut, shredded
1 scoop of stevia

For Rolling:

Almonds
Coconut oil
Spare coconut, shredded

Directions

1. Over low-heat settings in a large pan; heat the unsalted butter until completely melted.
2. Once done; add in the ricotta; giving everything a good stir until ricotta completely melts.
3. Slowly add 1/3 cup of shredded coconut and a tiny scoop of stevia; mix well.
4. Add psyllium husk; give everything a good stir until evenly mixed.
5. Add vanilla extract and the cardamom; continue to mix until the ingredients start forming a dough ball, for a couple of minutes.
6. Turn the heat off & set the mixture aside. Let cool at room temperature for 10 minutes.
7. In the meantime; set up a plate or tray. A plate or tray with baking paper over the top.
8. Once you can handle the mixture easily; coat your fingertips lightly with the coconut oil & roll a small quantity into a ball; pressing an almond inside the ball or roll into the shredded coconut & place the coated ball on the plate. Place in a refrigerator or fridge and let chill until set. Serve and enjoy.

CHOCOLATE CHERRY FAT BOMBS

Prep Time: 15 minutes
Cooking Time: 1 hour & 25 minutes
Servings: 6

Nutritional Info (Estimated Amount Per Serving)

176 Calories
146 Calories from Fat
15g Total Fat
14g Saturated Fat
0g Trans Fat
0.2g Polyunsaturated Fat
0.8g Monounsaturated Fat
0mg Cholesterol
4.2mg Sodium
90mg Potassium
9.5g Total Carbohydrates
2.8g Dietary Fiber
3.2g Sugars
1.7g Protein

Ingredients

¼ cup coconut oil, warm & melted
½ tsp. almond extract
3 tbsp. cacao powder
¾ cup dark sweet cherries, frozen & thawed
5 drops of liquid stevia
¼ cup melted coconut butter
½ tsp. vanilla extract

Directions

1. Mix the ingredients together (don't add the dark cherries at this point) in a large-sized bowl until mixed evenly. Now, mash the thawed dark cherries using a large fork & mix them with the chocolate mixture (it's important that you add the cherries along with their accumulated juices).
2. Fill an ice cube tray with the prepared mixture (filling each cube with approximately 1 tbsp. of the mixture) and let freeze until completely set. Store in an air-tight container in a fridge until ready to serve.

STRAWBERRY CHEESECAKE FAT BOMBS

Prep Time: 10 minutes
Cooking Time: 2 hours & 30 minutes
Servings: 6

Nutritional Information (Estimated Amount Per Serving)

193 Calories
171 Calories from Fat
19g Total Fat
13g Saturated Fat
0g Trans Fat
0.6g Polyunsaturated Fat
3.2g Monounsaturated Fat
29mg Cholesterol
124mg Sodium
64mg Potassium
390g Total Carbohydrates
0.3g Dietary Fiber
2.1g Sugars
1.9g Protein

Ingredients

¾ cup cream cheese, softened (5.3 oz)
½ cup strawberries, fresh or frozen (2.5 oz); washed & green parts removed
¼ cup butter (cut into small pieces) or coconut oil, softened (2 oz)
½ to 1 tbsp. vanilla extract or 1 vanilla bean
10–15 drops of liquid stevia

Directions

1. Place the coconut oil or butter and cream cheese in to a large-sized mixing bowl; set aside at room temperature until softened.
2. In the meantime, place the strawberries into a bowl; place in a blender for a smooth texture or mash them well using a fork.
3. Add the vanilla extract and stevia; mix well. Before you add & mix the strawberries with the leftover ingredients, ensure that they are at room temperature.
4. Add them to the bowl with cream cheese and softened butter.

5. Use a food processor or hand whisk; mix until combined well.
6. Fill small candy molds molds or muffin silicon with the prepared mixture. Place in the freezer until completely set, for a couple of hours.
7. After 2 hours, unmold the fat bombs & place them in a container. Keep the container in a freezer until ready to serve.

KETO FAT BOMB PUMPKIN PIE PATTIES

Prep Time: 15 minutes
Cooking Time: 1 hour & 10 minutes
Servings: 24

Nutritional Information (Estimated Amount Per Serving)

103 Calories
89 Calories from Fat
9.9g Total Fat
8.5g Saturated Fat
0g Trans Fat
0.1g Polyunsaturated Fat
0.5g Monounsaturated Fat
0mg Cholesterol
28mg Sodium
64mg Potassium
2.9g Total Carbohydrates
1.8g Dietary Fiber
0.9g Sugars
1.7g Protein

Ingredients

1 cup unsweetened coconut, long shredded
¼ tsp. pure vanilla extract, alcohol-free
25 drops of stevia extract, alcohol-free
¾ cup pumpkin puree, unsweetened
1 tbsp. ground cinnamon
¼ cup collagen, grass-fed
1 ½ tsp. ground ginger
½ cup coconut oil
A pinch of ground cloves
¼ tsp. Himalayan rock salt

Directions

1. Line a large-sized baking sheet with two standard-sized mini muffin silicon molds (with 12-count each); set aside.
2. Add coconut oil then shredded coconut, salt and stevia to the food processor. Process on high settings until drippy, for 6 to 8 minutes; scrapping the chunky bits from the side of your bowl as required.
3. Once smooth, set aside approximately ¼ cup of the prepared coconut mixture. Add the leftover ingredients to the bowl of your food processer (with the remaining coconut mixture) & process again until smooth and you get apple sauce like consistency, preferably on high-settings.
4. Evenly divide the mixture into the prepared muffin cups. Using the back of a spoon or with fingers; pressing down the mixture until completely flat. Top with the leftover white coconut mixture. Place the baking sheet to a freezer & let chill for an hour.
5. Serve and enjoy.

25523003R00052